ARTAUD AT RODEZ

ARTAUd AT RODEZ

CHARLES MAROWITZ

MARION BOYARS · LONDON

First published in Great Britain in 1977
by Marion Boyars Publishers Ltd, 18 Brewer Street, London W1R 4AS

A Marion Boyars Book
distributed by
Calder & Boyars Ltd, 18 Brewer Street, London W1R 4AS

In the United States by
Drama Book Specialists, 150 West 52nd Street, New York, N.Y. 10019

All performing rights in this play are strictly reserved and applications for
performances should be made to
The Open Space Theatre, 303 Euston Road, London NW1

No performance of this play may be given unless a licence
has been obtained prior to rehearsal

ISBN 0 7145 2631 2 Cased Edition
ISBN 0 7145 2632 0 Paperback Edition

Acknowledgement
THE ANTONIN ARTAUD AFFAIR: WHAT SHOULD BE KNOWN originally
published as AFFAIRE ANTONIN ARTAUD - CE QU'IL FAUT SAVOIR and
I LOOKED AFTER ANTONIN ARTAUD originally published as J'AI SOIGNE
ANTONIN ARTAUD in No 63-64 of LA TOUR DE FEU - ANTONIN ARTAUD
OU LA SANTE DES POETES, December 1959 by Pierre Boujut, 16200
Jarnac, France

Set by Gilbert Composing Services
Leighton Buzzard
Printed in Great Britain by
Whitstable Litho, Whitstable

CONTENTS

Introduction   7

ARTAUD AT RODEZ (Play)   11

Appendices

Conversation with Gaston Ferdière   67

Conversation with Roger Blin   75

Conversation with Arthur Adamov   82

*The Antonin Artaud Affair:
What should be known
by Marie-Ange Malausséna*   89

*I Looked After Antonin Artaud
by Dr. Gaston Ferdière*   103

INTRODUCTION

My own awareness of Antonin Artaud dates from 1958. By some means, I no longer remember how, I came across *The Theatre and its Double.* I found its tone of voice mesmerizing. I was being hectored by a sensibility which had seen something very special and very different in the theatre, and the insistence of that vision, rather than its clarity, was riveting.

Around 1963, in the pages of *Encore* Magazine and in private conversations with Peter Brook, I tried to chart the labyrinthine course of Artaud's thought and how it could be practically applied. I knew that Artaud himself had not applied it. His *Cenci*, for instance, had been a crude failure staged in an unremarkable surrealist convention, and his earlier experiments, the programmes of the THEATRE ALFRED JARRY, although fervently proseltyzed, had not produced any tangible body of work from which aesthetic principles could be formulated. In his own opinion, his cancelled radio-play *Pour Finir avec le Jugement de Dieu* was the work most representative of his Theatre of Cruelty, but as this was a verse-play for four voices interspersed with cries and bits of percussion, it wasn't the kind of thing from which one could extrapolate theatrical notions. Odd pieces like *Spurt of Blood* and *The Philosopher's Stone* were murky bits of surrealist effluvia. Ultimately, all one had was the prose and the poetry; an exhortation to people who, like himself, wished to change the shape and feel of the contemporary theatre.

In 1966, Peter Brook and I put some of Artaud's ideas to the test. The THEATRE OF CRUELTY SEASON at the LAMDA theatre in London was not a reconstruction of Artaud's theatre; a theatre which, as I say, never really existed—but only a few random experiments informed by Artaud's aesthetic. Subsequently, in my adaptations of *Hamlet, Macbeth, Othello* and *The Shrew,* I sensed many of Artaud's ideas concerning classics and psychology burrowing away in my mind, and although no play can be said to be derivative of Artaud, I certainly acknowledge that the force of his polemic shaped my own convictions.

More fascinating than the ideas was the man himself and the tragic life he had led. At the start of the war, he was incarcerated in various mental asylums in France and then in 1942, his life reached a poignant climax when he was moved to Rodez and put under the jurisdiction of Dr. Gaston Ferdière. Here was a man of genius under the strict control of a man of science who, as it happened, was also a would-be poet and essayist. For me two very distinct (and opposed) world-views came into dynamic collision in this encounter and this prompted the writing of *Artaud at Rodez*. In the midsixties, preparing a radio-programme for the BBC, I had the opportunity to talk to many of Artaud's friends in Paris and secured an interview with Dr. Ferdière at which he spoke candidly of his association with Artaud. That association, ten years after Artaud's death, became the subject of a small-scale scandal in Paris and the issues of that controversy have been incorporated into the play. In addition to the script which was first performed at the Trastavere Theatre in Rome and subsequently at The Open Space in London, I have included some of the background material on which the play has been based.

A play is not a piece-of-journalism and consequently, doesn't contain the balance that exists in the best kind of news story. But despite certain innate prejudices, I have tried to be fair to all the characters that figured in Artaud's life—but as the work is non-naturilistic and subject to occasional flights-of-fancy, it is 'poetic' rather than 'literal' truth which is being sought. But even this is suspect. One can only talk about things the way one sees them, and in *Artaud at Rodez,* I have seen them *this* way. I realize, and the reader will quickly understand after perusing the material in the back of this book, there are many other ways of interpreting these incidents and many other conclusions that could be drawn. There is nothing 'authoritative' about this interpretation of events. On the other hand, it *is* derived from authoritative sources.

To say any more is to become mealy-mouthed.

Charles Marowitz

June 1977

ARTAUD AT RODEZ

CAST

Antonin Artaud	CLIVE MERRISON
Dr. Gaston Ferdière	RICHARD MAYES
Marie-Ange Malausséna Mrs. Ferdière, Iya Abdy	THELMA HOLT
Roger Blin	MALCOLM TIERNEY
Jacques Rivière Van Gogh, Reporter	BRIAN GWASPARI
Dullin, Beat Poet Dr. Dequeker	ROBERT OATES
Louis Jouvet Reporter	GEORGE IRVING
Muse, Bobby-soxer	LINDA HAYDEN

Directed by Charles Marowitz
Designed by Robin Don

First Performance Nov 28, 1976
Teatro a Trastavere. Rome

Sound of Artaud's Tarahumara Cry.

ARTAUD, *strapped to table, rapidly wheeled on
stage by* TWO DOCTORS. *Electrodes are fixed to
his head. Electricity applied. Tarahumara chants in
background. Sound of* FERDIERE's *soothing
voice—imposes itself over* TAPE.

FERDIERE: I shall be speaking tonight chiefly about
my period in Rodez where I first met Antonin
Artaud and began the long and complicated treatment of his peculiar case. But I should say at the
outset that Artaud was known to me long before
Rodez. We moved, in fact, in very much the same
circles; the post-surrealist, para-surrealist circles.
And more than once, I had been asked to take him
in hand. I was told, and I had no reason to doubt
it, that Artaud's behaviour had become increasingly
outrageous. He was given to unpredictable fits of
anger. He behaved odiously in society, and often
with an incoherence, that made his friends fear the
worst.

There was, for example, this walking-stick—
which was always with him, which he believed to
be descended from St. Patrick. And with this stick
he used to threaten harmless customers sitting
outside La Coupole or the Café Flore. It was quite
disgraceful, but people had come to accept this
kind of behaviour from him. Time and time again,
I was urged to take him in hand. But I refused—
consistently. Why? Because I myself was entirely
devoted to what you might call, poetic liberty.

I recall our first meeting very vividly. Of
course, it was some time ago now, in '41, I
believe . . . .

*(Lights up on surreal dinner table, entirely white,
like a soft sculpture.* MRS. FERDIERE, *holding
a lorgnette, sits immobile staring at* ARTAUD
who is opposite her, also motionless, eyes staring.

Beside ARTAUD *stands a traditional French maid, dressed in black, trimmed in white. In front of her, a tea-trolley, an all-white top contains glistening surgical instruments. During the scene she slowly polishes her instruments and replaces them in their positions on the trolley.)*

FERDIERE: Ah, oui. M'sieur Artaud Théatre de Cruaté; "Le Théatre et son Double". Rest assured, your fame has come before you. You are no stranger in our midst. In fact, I believe we have many acquaintances in common. M'sieur Breton, is I believe, known to you; and M'sieur Rivière is an old friend. *(Pause)* Unlike yourself, I have never quite achieved publication in the estimable Nouvelle Revue Française, but some of my modest little works have appeared in smaller select periodicals. Do you know Le Miroir? Or perhaps, Les Petites Affiches? *(Pause)* No? C'est dommage. In my younger days, I even did a touch of acting. Nothing very formidable, I can assure you. Church Hall Shakespeare. *(Pause)* "It is the cause, it is the cause my soul". *(Pause. Laughs nervously)* Of course, I am not primarily an artist, but a man of science? And yet you know, my wife has always encouraged my aesthetic pursuits. She is thoroughly convinced I could make as successful a career in poetry as I have in medicine. But you know what flatterers women are. *(Laughs nervously. Pause)*

    You know, despite appearances, we are quite alike in many ways you and I. You, grappling with the demons of your psyche to produce insights in poetry and prose; I, exploring the innermost depths of the mind, to purge those unruly shadows that darken the spirit of man. In a manner of speaking, we are almost, dare I say it, fellow-artists? . . . *(Ingration withers completely.)*

    My dear, do offer our guest a little claret.

(MRS. FERDIERE *downs lorgnettes and briskly offers decanter.* ARTAUD *falls to his knees and*

12

*begins chanting Tarahumara rituals, crossing himself,
etc.* MRS. FERDIERE, *hand still outstretched,
looks at* DR. FERDIERE *who, wincing, looks at*
ARTAUD *then back to his wife. Gives a signal.*
ARTAUD *is removed by two white jacketed*
DOCTORS. *Sound of* ARTAUD's *voice on* TAPE.
*French actor arrives reciting Racine declaiming
in Comédie Française style.* FRENCH PRIEST
confesses ARTAUD, *confession turns into blow
job. French actor adopts* PRIEST's *confessional
stance.* PRIEST *begins to declaim Racine [or "O
for a Muse of fire"].* TWO ACTORS *march out,
throw a rich tapestry over themselves, kneel down
and become a dais.* JACQUES RIVIERE, *spouting
Artaud's correspondence, sits on a dais.* PRIEST
pushes ARTAUD *down at his feet, spreadeagled
like a penitent. All of these actions are simultaneous
ending with* RIVIERE *sitting and* ARTAUD 's
final spreadeagled position.)

RIVIERE: *(Tearing up poems and scattering them over*
ARTAUD *as he speaks)* I have read attentively
that which you were kind enough to submit to my
judgement. There are in your poems, as I told you
before, awkwardnesses and above all, strangenesses
that are disconcerting. But they seem to me to
correspond to a certain studied effort on your
part rather than to a lack of command in your
thought. Obviously, this prevents me, for the
moment, from publishing any of your poems in
the Nouvelle Revue Française. You do not attain,
in general, to a sufficient unity of impression. But
with a little patience, you will succeed in writing
perfectly coherent and harmonious poems.
    I shall always be delighted to see you, to talk
with you and to read whatever it pleases you to
submit to me.

(ARTAUD *rises, struggles with* PRIEST, *and
finally makes it to* RIVIERE. RIVIERE *gives
signal for him to speak. All goes still.)*

13

ARTAUD: I suffer from a frightful illness of the mind. My thought abandons me at every level. From the simple fact of thought to the external fact of its materialization into words. Words, forms of phrases, inner directions of the mind, simple reactions of the mind—I am in constant pursuit of my intellectual being. Thus when I *can* seize a form, imperfect though it is, I put it down in the fear of losing the thought. I do not do myself justice, I know: I suffer from this, but I depend on it for fear of not dying completely.

RIVIERE: *(After Pause)* Would you like me to return the volume you so kindly provided?

ARTAUD: *(Not being understood)* I am a man who has suffered much from the mind, and for this reason I have the right to speak.

(Cut to MARIE-ANGE MALAUSSENA, a black veiled figure in mourning. ALL OTHERS exit.)

MARIE-ANGE: Antonin, Mama is dead.

ARTAUD: Mama?

MARIE-ANGE: The scandal and the gossip have killed her.

ARTAUD: Mama?

MARIE-ANGE: Mother, Antonin. Mother!

ARTAUD: *(Mechanically)* I, Antonin Artaud, born September 4, 1896 at Marseille, 4 rue Jardin des Plantes, out of a uterus I had nothing to do with and which I have never had a thing to do with even previously, for this is no way to be born, to be copulated and masturbated for nine months by the membrane, the yawning membrane which tooth-lessly devours, as the Upanishads say, and I know that I was born otherwise, born of my own works and not of a mother . . .

MARIE-ANGE: Don't talk nonsense, Antonin. Mother

14

is dead and you killed her. You, your friends, your circle, your godlessness.

ARTAUD;   I am one with Jesus; I am of Jesus; I am Jesus' own.

FERDIERE: His delirium, I fear, will never entirely be cured. Whilst he is a threat to society, society must be defended against him. One day, perhaps, who can tell.

MARIE-ANGE: Oh, bless you, Doctor. Keep him from us, as long as he lives. Keep him in this sanctuary where he may yet rediscover God.

FERDIERE: Never fear, Mme. Malaussena. We know how to treat artists at Rodez.

(ARTAUD abruptly returns to RIVIERE's dais)

RIVIERE: An idea has occurred to me which I resisted for some time, but which I now find definitely attractive. Why not publish the letters you have written to me? I have just re-read the one of January 29th and it is really quite remarkable. We could give the writer and recipient invented names, if you like. Perhaps too, we could introduce an excerpt from your poems. The whole thing might form a little novel in letters which might be quite curious.

ARTAUD: *(After a pause, pretentiously)* Yes, your idea pleases me, it gladdens me, it gratifies me. But on condition that it gives whoever reads us, the impression that he is not being presented with something that has been fabricated. Why lie? Why try to place on the literary level a thing which is the very cry of life? The reader must be provided with all the material for discussion.

(ALL make a circle around ARTAUD, simulating the activity of adoring journalists; one with a sketch pad; one with a flash camera; a GIRL dressed in an Artaud tee-shirt. ROGER BLIN

dresses ARTAUD *in crushed black hat and black cape; hands him a shillelagh.* ARTAUD, *now transformed into a celebrity, plays to the* CROWD.)

ARTAUD: A man possesses himself in flashes.

MARIE-ANGE: He was always a poseur.

ARTAUD: . . . and even when he does not possess himself.

MARIE-ANGE: Even as a child.

ARTAUD: He does not quite attain himself.

JOURNALIST 1: Charlatan.

ARTAUD: I can truly say that I am not in this world . . .

MARIE-ANGE: He's never really been well.

ARTAUD: And this is not merely a mental attitude.

JOURNALIST 2: Playing at madness . . .

JOURNALIST 1: As he played at genius . . .

ARTAUD: It is an actual sickness that affects my soul in its deepest reality . . .

JOURNALIST 2: One has to humour him, I suppose.

ARTAUD: The poison of being!

MARIE-ANGE: It was quite endearing when he was six.

(ALL *stop. Begin to ape* ARTAUD'S *manner while* ARTAUD *now speaks quietly and with sincerity, their jeers progressively mounting.* BLIN *suddenly intervenes.*)

ARTAUD: My whole life is shot through with petty doubts and uncertainties . . . my weaknesses are of an even more tremulous nature . . . Nebulous and ill-formulated . . . They have live roots . . . Roots of anguish that reach to the heart of life . . .

16

BLIN: *(Rescuing* ARTAUD *from others)* What do
you, or anyone, know of the artistic sensibility?
You are always there with your taunts and your
dismissals. "Charlatan!" "Poseur!" "Fraud".
With such words you tried to drive your rusty
little nails into Jarry, Baudelaire, Duchamp,
Picasso! You are the sworn enemies of art—
until afterwards, when you can comfortably
derive its benefits, in the cinema, on television,
in your cosy, suburban drawing-rooms.
(Ferociously) Do not dare to despise what you
cannot understand.

(ONE OF THE CROWD *frozen in his tableau
suddenly snaps his fingers as if commencing
rehearsal. Tableau dissolves.* TWO OF THEM
becoming actors in DULLIN'S *rehearsal.)*

DULLIN: All right, ladies and gentlemen. We shall
take it from the top of Scene 3—where the
Emperor Charlemagne, M'sieur Artaud,—I
hope you are feeling better today? Um. Good.
Good—Where Charlemagne enters and sits on the
throne. Quiet, please. Take your places. And,
M'sieur Artaud—you enter.

(ARTAUD, *on all fours, lopes towards the throne
and after much to-do, sits.)*

DULLIN: *(Uncertain—not wishing to cause a scene)*
Yes, well, that was fine, M'sieur Artaud, but
perhaps we could try that entrance again—a little
less . . . um . . . stylized. (ARTAUD *slowly,
smouldering, exits.*) All right, please—and entrée.

(ARTAUD, *now loping like a wounded animal,
moves towards the throne and after much to-do,
sits.)*

DULLIN: *(Sensing the danger)* Yes, well. Um,
perhaps we could try that just once more . . . a
little more . . . fluently . . . perhaps. Yes, with a
little more fluency. (ARTAUD *smouldering, exists.*)
Positions, and entrée.

17

(ARTAUD *in a grotesquely caricatured walk which is still more a slump than a walk, makes it to the throne, and sits.*)

DULLIN: M'sieur Artaud—could we not simply have you enter from the wings, walk to the throne, and sit?

ARTAUD: *(Enraged)* Oh well, if it's realism you're after! *(Knocks over throne and strides out)*

DULLIN: *(After* ARTAUD'S *stormy exit—to* OTHERS) Ten minute break.

(After a moment ARTAUD *returns, now cowed and apologetic.)*

ARTAUD: M. Dullin . . .

(DULLIN *shuts his script and walks off haughtily.* ARTAUD *stands a crumpled figure. As* ROGER BLIN *enters, he slowly raises himself up to his previous posture.* BLIN *approaches with excessive respect.*)

ARTAUD: Roger, I am plotting a revolution of sensibility. Will you follow me?

BLIN: Anywhere!

ARTAUD: It will be a slow, dangerous course. We will be abused, spurned—even tortured. But once begun, there can be no turning back.

BLIN: You can rely on me. *(Gives* ARTAUD *his hand.)*

ARTAUD: *(Clasping it warmly)* Good, good. We will need provisions, equipment, weapons, strategies—do you have fifty francs on you?

BLIN: Yes.

ARTAUD: Good. The first step is some absinthe. That will clear the head for other things.

BLIN: *(Inspired)* We shall do it, Antonin . . . . We shall do it together.

18

ARTAUD: *(After an examination)* Roger . . .

BLIN: *(Prompt)* Yes.

ARTAUD: You're not putting me on, are you?

BLIN: *(Confused)* I don't understand.

ARTAUD: You do believe me, don't you?

BLIN: *(Incredulous it can be questioned)* Of course I do.

ARTAUD: Do you have those rare, shit-eating qualities that make a true protege?

BLIN: *(Steadfast)* I hope so.

ARTAUD: All the necessary qualifications?

BLIN: *(Fervent)* Try me!

ARTAUD: Blind obedience?

(BLIN *bows his head down in a short, sharp movement.)*

Unswerving devotion?

(BLIN *snaps up his head, his expression radiating devotion.*

Unquestioning loyalty?

(BLIN *embraces* ARTAUD *suddenly, and hugs him to his bosom.)*

A private income?

BLIN: *(Releasing him suddenly)* For years I have been looking for someone in whom I can completely submerge myself. An idol—with or without feet of clay—it makes not difference. I am the kind of man who can only shine in the shadows. Will you permit me to cling to your shirt-tails?

ARTAUD: *(Emotionally, clasping BLIN to bosom)* The first disciple! I need only eleven more.

19

(ARTAUD *releases* BLIN *and takes one step back. The two men look adoringly at each other as* DR. FERDIERE, *already continuing his lecture, walks between them and into the next scene.*)

FERDIERE: Under the provisions of the law of 1838, a somewhat ancient law but under which, in France, we classify madness, it is prescribed that people who are dangerous are to be certified as such. Now Artaud had been, and always was, in the truest sense a dangerous man. A man from whom society had the duty to protect itself. He had gone to Ireland, as you may remember, to retrace the footsteps of St. Patrick. Just as a few years before, he had gone to Mexico in search of ancient Indian gods. We know that in August of 1937, he was in Dublin—without money, barely able to speak English, but very much in possession of his magical cane. We know that a few days before he set sail for France, he created a scandal at a Jesuit College, chanting his Tarahumara Indian rituals during Holy Mass. The police were called; he was forcibly ejected, and on board the Washington, very much against his will; alone, somewhat hunted and . . .

ARTAUD: Sitting by the porthole, watching the sea undulate slowly as if it were lapping a message in code against the window.

(A STEWARD *and a* MECHANIC *with a monkey-wrench enter casually.*)

STEWARD: Excuse me, sir. We've just got a little problem with the ventilation system. Won't take a minute.

(ARTAUD *terrified. Raises up his cane*)

ARTAUD: I know you, demons. I can smell the brimstone on your shoes. Back, back! *(Brandishes the cane)*

MECHANIC: *(Aside)* 'e's round the twist, if y' ask me.

STEWARD: You see, M'sieur, we only want to . . .

ARTAUD: *(Brandishing cane, strikes out with it)*
           Back, back! I have been warned of your coming.

MECHANIC: Nutty as a fruitcake.

           (ARTAUD *swings out at* MECHANIC *with his
           cane. There is a scuffle. Cries for help. "We've
           got a nut here."* DOCTOR *enters, sees the
           altercation, returns with straightjacket.*

           ARTAUD *is trussed up and placed in isolation—
           while on* TAPE.)

VOICE: February 12, 1937. Office of the French
          Consul, Dublin. Paragraph. "The Irish police made
          Monsieur Artaud's presence in Dublin known to
          the French Legation. We expressed the desire of
          sending our compatriot who was without resources
          and in a state of high exaltation, back to France.
          "The Legation intervened as much as possible in
          favour of M'sieur Artaud who embarked at Cobh
          on September 29, on the Washington, and must
          have arrived the following morning at Le Havre.
          As we have heard no more of the incident, we
          assume all was resolved to everyone's
          satisfaction."

          (ARTAUD *and his* MUSE. THE MUSE *very like
          Jean Harlow—blonde, beautiful, long slinky
          white dress.)*

ARTAUD: At last you've come. Where have you
           been? Don't you realize what they've been doing
           to me?

MUSE: Artists are supposed to suffer. Don't you
         ever go to the cinema?

ARTAUD: But I was just getting started. The Cenci
           had just opened.

MUSE: And closed, rather promptly, I believe.

ARTAUD: That was your fault. Where were you

when I needed you. To help with the actors, with the set, with the menopaustic twat who kept walking into the scenery.

MUSE: I'm not at your beck and call, you know. Paul Valéry had need of me as well—not to mention Paul Claudel.

ARTAUD: You were with *him,* you gutless bitch. You forsook me to spend time with that putrid, papal horse's ass?

MUSE: A Muse must share herself around.

ARTAUD: So does a whore, you contemptible slut!

MUSE: Your treatment doesn't seem to be doing you much good, darling. You're as erratic as ever.

ARTAUD: My treatment? My imprisonment! My bondage! I've called for you from the very first day in Cobh, then again at Dun Laoghaire, and again at Ville-Evrard. How could you be so cruel—so inhuman.

MUSE: But muses *are* inhuman. Really, Antoine, you are so droll.

ARTAUD: My name is Antonin—not Antoine.

MUSE: I'm sorry. What did I say?

ARTAUD: How could you do this to me?

MUSE: Really, darling, you're sounding more like a discarded lover every day. Aren't you glad to see me?

ARTAUD: Have you brought it?

MUSE: Would I come without it? Is there any point at all in being a Muse without providing inspiration? Of course I've brought it. I knew you were lost without it. *(Slowly raises dress to reveal garter. In garter, small pipe)* Here, Antonin, take it while you can. It's very rare, you know. Not easy to

22

come by in these grim black market days. Make the most of it.

(She helps him puff smoke. He becomes euphoric. Looks up to MUSE, sings weakly and plaintively)

ARTAUD: They asked me how I knew
           My true love was true
           I of course replied
           Something here inside
           Cannot be denied.

           Now laughing friends deride
           Tears I cannot hide
           So I smile and say
           When a lovely flame dies
           Smoke gets in your eyes.

(MUSIC of "SMOKE GETS IN YOUR EYES" wells up. ARTAUD and MUSE dance to it like Astaire and Rogers.)

FERDIERE: *(Lecturing)* You see, in the madness of Artaud there was a kind of combat, a gigantic combat, a Manichean combat between God and the devil. And it was sometimes God who triumphed and made of Artaud a man consumed with a burning faith, going to Mass several times a week spending hours with the Almoner of the hospital— and at other times, a person who was prey to the devil who insulted passing women and spat on imaginary people . . . and for this reason I cannot, as M. François Mauriac does, make a great mystic of Artaud. I would have to make him a great mystic and a great madman in the same breath. Now, at our last meeting . . .

(Cut to ARTAUD with LOUIS JOUVET dressed in traditional Louis XIV costume, cosmeticized with beauty marks, standing upstage facing away.)

ARTAUD: And I am honoured to have had the confidence of Louis Jouvet. But you must feel

as I do, as everyone does today, that we can go
further, that the true theatre we are all waiting
for implies a complete reversal of standards, of
framework, of orientation; its centre of gravity
is elsewhere. And it seems to me, if you ever
intend to vary your productions, that among these
conformist plays you should introduce others that
are more decidedly and essentially revolutionary.

(JOUVET *turns slowly with an irritable expression
on his face. As soon as* ARTAUD *makes to speak,*
JOUVET *raises up his hand for silence, then
launches into exaggerated speech in French*
[Racine].)

ARTAUD: . . . My notion is that one has to play
along with the times in order to be revolutionary;
it is the only way to commercial success.

(JOUVET *kisses* ARTAUD *on both cheeks. As
soon as* ARTAUD *tries to return the embrace,*
JOUVET *breaks away still spouting classical
French text,* ARTAUD *follows on hands and
knees, and during next speech, crawls on top of*
JOUVET *and sits on his thigh.*)

ARTAUD: I am taking the liberty of reminding you
of our plan for an appointment after your return
from travels at the end of July. If I seem to be
clinging or tenacious, it is only because I have the
impression that I have something to say about the
impermeability of the stage-world to anything that
does not strictly belong to it, about the quasi-
uselessness of language which is not the vehicle
but the stitch of thought. I am not a businessman,
and if I have enough to live on, I don't care about
anything else.

(JOUVET *turns angrily to* ARTAUD *and flips
him off; resumes French text.*)

(Pitiably) Please try to understand the spirit of
what I am saying. What I need is a helping hand,
to allow me to exercise my ability, which I do not

think is without interest, and if one admits I
have something to say, let me start mumbling it.
I am much easier to get along with than they say,
I beg you to believe in the urgency of the help
I am asking you for.

(ARTAUD *springs up Kung-Fu fashion and moves
as if to assault* JOUVET.)

(Haughtily) Since I have had no word from you
about any of my plans, I hereby request that
you return all my manuscripts.
    Once I take the trouble to convey even a
sketch of my ideas to someone, I do not permit
my communications to remain without answer or
discussion. For that matter, I am about to carry
out elsewhere these projects, that I couldn't put
into execution with you, and it will be your loss.

(JOUVET *turns to* ARTAUD *who immediately
grovels before him and takes his hand.)*

(Fawning) When can you see me? I have a play
I want to read to you, not to reveal its beauties,
that would be absurd. But so that you may hear
my interpretation, to suggest to you my personal
resonance. Please give my a definite appointment
. . . Has the Pigalle Theatre really accepted THE
KING OF THE CHILDREN? What kind of
success can it possibly hope for? I simply do not
understand.

(JOUVET *slaps* ARTAUD'S *cheek with his
glove)*

(Hedging) My personal opinion of the value of
the play counts for little. I simply wanted to know
whether it was definite that this play will be put
on and whether you, Louis Jouvet, personally
expected it to be a success. *(Pause)* And what
kind of success could you possibly expect with it.

(JOUVET *slaps other cheek with same glove.)*

I also wanted to know if the opening date had been definitely decided. If . . .

(JOUVET *continues to look steadily at* ARTAUD *and then . . .*

JOUVET *throws down the gauntlet.*)

ARTAUD: *(Utterly contrite)* I am sincerely and cordially at your service for anything you expect of me for THE KING OF THE CHILDREN. I am not at the moment in a position to refuse employment and I am asking only that you give me an opportunity to work.

(JOUVET *bends down, proffers his backside.* ARTAUD *bends down, kisses his ass.*)

JOURNALISTS: *(Kissing)* Viva L'Athenée! Vive la Comédie Française, Vive la France!

(JOUVET *lifts* ARTAUD *on to his shoulders.*

THREE JOURNALISTS *have appeared. Avid, highly-impressed reporters with* ARTAUD *who behaves like a celebrity.*)

QUESTION: M. Artaud, in the cultrual history of France, where precisely is your place?

ARTAUD: In the forefront.

QUESTION: Ah, the avant-garde.

ARTAUD: "Avant garde is French for bullshit?"

QUESTION: La Rochefoucauld?

ARTAUD: Jean Lenn'on!

(JOUVET *unburdens himself of* ARTAUD, *crosses downstage right, centre of a tableau created by the* THREE REPORTERS.)

QUESTION: Do you believe your place in posterity is secure?

26

ARTAUD: I am not even certain of my hotel-room, mon ami. Posterity . . . *(Hunches shoulders)*

QUESTION: M. François Mauriac has called you a saint; one of God's very own.

ARTAUD: He is always name-dropping.

QUESTION: Other critics have not been quite so appreciative. The general consensus is that either you are a fraud or a madman.

ARTAUD: If a fraud then in the hallowed tradition of French culture; if a madman, then in keeping with the spirit of the times.

(REPORTERS *suddenly break tableau and reform in new tableau opposite side of stage.)*

QUESTION: I believe that in your theories, you have said the theatre is like the plague?

ARTAUD: Metaphorically speaking.

QUESTION: Metaphorically?

ARTAUD: Yes, as one might say, journalism is what literature does when it defecates.

(REPORTERS *break tableau and reform on opposite side of stage.* ARTAUD *leaping into their arms where he reclines as if on a chaise-longue.)*

QUESTION: *(Uncertainly)* Your Theatre Alfred Jarry, after a great burst of publicity, played only four programmes to very small audiences. Was that a disappointment?

ARTAUD: Not at all. By being a pathetic failure, witnessed by only a handful of people, it now has the opportunity to become a legend about which millions will disagree. A success would never have permitted that degree of notoriety.

QUESTION: But surely you would have preferred a success?

27

ARTAUD: What, and destroy the consistency of a
          lifetime?

          (REPORTERS *break tableau, create a cradle with*
          hands on which ARTAUD *can sit and is hoisted*
          up in the air.)

QUESTION/ALL: What is the Theatre of Cruelty?

ARTAUD: *(Pause)* Imagine, if you will, the last
          scene of Hamlet, when the stage is strewn with
          corpses and the audience is tumultuous with
          applause.

          (JOURNALISTS *toss* ARTAUD *downstage, then*
          kneel before him giving rapt attention.)

          Imagine then, the curtains part and not one actor
          rises for a curtain-call. Imagine a doctor scrambles
          up to the stage with a stethoscope in his trembling
          fingers and applies the ear of the instrument to the
          hearts of all the fallen actors. Imagine the audience
          spellbound and hushed as they might be at an
          acrobatic act that had suddenly gone wrong.
          Picture the doctor shaking his head forlornly, and
          the curtains hurriedly drawing closed. No words.
          No explanation—only the agonizing silence of the
          living tipping back their seats and rustling their
          programmes as the unmistakeable stench of death
          wafts itself from the other side of the curtains
          into the paralyzed auditorium.

QUESTION: M'sieur Artaud, you are noted from one
          end of Paris to the other as a purveyor of black
          humour. But can you tell me, what is black
          humour like?

          (ARTAUD *slowly removes switch blade from*
          back pocket; opens it and places blade just under
          his hair-line as if it gives him temporary relief
          from some excruciating pain. After a static
          moment, he suddenly slashes REPORTER's
          throat.)

ARTAUD: Like that!

(Dead REPORTER *is hastily dragged out.*
ARTAUD *strides off in opposite direction.)*

FERDIERE: *(Lecturing)* Well here is Artaud at
Rodez. In sympathetic surroundings; with food,
cigarettes, privacy. A special patient at a time of
great strife when everyone is suffering deprivations.
And yet, he remains stagnant; inert; inactive. But
this is no ordinary patient, but the author of Le
Théatre et Son Double, a force in the avant garde.
A man who was going to revolutionize the theatre.
And so I feel it incumbent upon myself to do
something; to jolt him out of his lethargy; to
make him functional once more.

(ARTAUD *sitting on a hospital stool, beside him*
DR. FERDIERE's *tubular chair.)*

FERDIERE: You disappoint me. I must say, my dear
Artaud, as much as it grieves me to say it, you
sorely disappoint me.
      You sit, you eat, you bathe, you sleep. Every
part of you that confirms your physical, biological
existence, functions. But your artist's soul? That
is nowhere to be seen. *(Pause)* You're tired, I know,
Dispirited, melancholic. I understand you very well,
dear friend. I can appreciate the lassitude of an
exhausted artist. I know only too well . . .
      But you must remember what people expect
from you. The war will not last forever. And what
then? You must return. You must *be* returned.
You must, like the phoenix rising from its ashes,
soar again—into the buoyant cameradie of the
Deux Magots and the Café Flore.
      You are part of the culture of France, and it
is to the culture of France that you must return.
      Renewed.
      Rediscovered.
      Reborn!

(ARTAUD *stands on stool behind* FERDIERE

29

and proceeds to strangle him.

On TAPE, *coinciding with* FERDIERE*'s open-mouthed silent cry, the* SOUND *of* ARTAUD*'s tarahumara cry. At end of cry,* FERDIERE *slumps to floor;* ARTAUD *retains static position on stool, cigarette hanging from his lips.*

Nothing happens for 20 seconds. Gradually FERDIERE *slowly rises up from the floor, takes up "Alice in Wonderland" and sits in his chair.*

Simultaneously ARTAUD *climbs slowly down from stool, picks up pad and sits like a child on his stool.*

FERDIERE *slowly rises and begins to read "Alice in Wonderland" in English.* ARTAUD *translates like a child into French.)*

FERDIERE: *(Colourfully)* Once upon a time there were three little sisters, the dormouse began in a great hurry . . .

ARTAUD: *(Dully)* "Il y avait une fois trois petites soeurs, commença la loir voluble . . .

FERDIERE: "and their names were Elsie, Lacie and Tilli . . ."

ARTAUD: "nommées Elsie, Julie et Tilli . . ."

FERDIERE: "And they lived at the bottom of a well . . . "

ARTAUD: "Elles vivaient au fond d'un puits . . ."

FERDIERE: "What did they live on", said Alice, who always took a great interest in questions of eating and drinking.

ARTAUD: "De quoi vivaient-elles", demanda Alice, toujours très interessée à la question du boire et du manger . . .

FERDIERE: "They lived on treacle", said the
              Dormouse after thinking a minute or two.

ARTAUD: "Le loir reflêchit une minute ou deux;
              puis: — "Elles vivaient de sirop".

FERDIERE: "They couldn't have done that, you
              know", Alice gently remarked.

ARTAUD: "Elles ne l'auraient pas pus, voyons, fit
              doucement remarquer Alice . . .

FERDIERE: "They'd have been ill."

              *(Pause. ARTAUD doesn't reply. FERDIERE
              repeats.)*

FERDIERE: "They'd have been ill."

ARTAUD: "Elles se seraient rendue malades."

FERDIERE: "So they were," said the Dormouse.
              Very, very, ill."

ARTAUD: "Aussi l'étaient-elles, très, très malades."

*(ARTAUD throws down book and rises
threateningly. Confronts FERDIERE, who
likewise confronts him. TWO white-jacketed
DOCTORS holding whips appear behind
ARTAUD. In background dull electrical
SOUND throbs menacingly.*

*ARTAUD and FERDIERE confront each other—
western-style duel. FERDIERE makes a small
tight gesture with both hands that ends with a
downward position of the head. Then turns to
ARTAUD. ARTAUD makes a flamboyant
version of the same gesture. DOCTORS lash
him. FERDIERE makes the same gesture again.
Turns to ARTAUD. ARTAUD makes his own
flamboyant gesture. He is lashed even harder.
FERDIERE makes his gesture again. Then repeats
it. Then turns to ARTAUD. ARTAUD
tentatively begins to make the same gesture,
but ends with head turned upward instead of*

31

downward. He is lashed again. FERDIERE
*approaches him, puts his hand to his chin and
looks him squarely in the eye, then proceeds to
repeat the gesture. Then steps back and awaits*
ARTAUD'S *repetition.*

ARTAUD *begins very tentatively, very slowly to
repeat gesture. Gets it right. Then turns to*
FERDIERE *who demonstrates the last downward
head-turn.*

ARTAUD *repeats this.* DOCTORS *embrace*
ARTAUD *approvingly.* FERDIERE *holds out
his hand,* ARTAUD *clasps it and begins intoning
in a monotonous frenzy of adulation.)*

ARTAUD: You are the divine, electric sensibility.
Without you, I would be a vegetable. Was a
vegetable. You not only helped me to live. You
invited me to live, you dug me from my grave.
Without your aid, without your kindness, without
your solicitation, I am nothing. A man without a
private room. Without tobacco. Without chocolate.
Without laudanum. Without hope. Persevere with
me, I beg of you, saintly doctor, holy magician,
healer, soother, saviour. *(Repeats)*

(BLIN *watches the display with disgust.* DR. D.
turns defiantly to him.)

DR.D: *(To* BLIN) You are an artist, I know, and your
ivory castle is splendid and impregnable. But what
do you know of survival? What do you remember
of the war. Of the occupation? When Frenchmen
murdered for bread and cigarettes. When hunger
gnawed at every belly, and inmates from Chezal-
Benoit and St. Anne starved to death by the
thousands. Poor, pathetic trembling maniacs who
had learned to live with their demons, but could
not understand this sudden cruel withdrawal of
the very sustenance that allowed their delirium to
exist. As they shovelled these raving, wretched,
half-starved, oblivious madmen into their shallow

32

graves, one man, above all, sat comfortably in a
room, in a wing, separate from all the others, in
the safety of Rodez. His cigarettes beside him; his
snuff and his chewing-tobacco. His Baudelaire and
his Lautréament. His parcels from home and his
special coterie of doctors to keep his artistic
delirium in tact. Do not talk to me of Artaud
the poet, Artaud the visionary. Without us,
without Ferdière, there would have been only a
skeleton with eyes like billiard-balls and a little
unmarked mound of earth to signify that among
this horde of mindless dead, there was one,
demented poet who, before the war, had gained
the attention of a handful of surrealists, now
long gone.

*(Short drum roll and cymbal crash. BARKER
dressed in broad music hall outfit breaks through
tableau. In background ARTAUD and IYA ABDY
mime according to BARKER'S description.)*

MC: Ladies and gentlemen, roll up, roll up—for the
event of the century, "The Cenci!" A play so
barbaric, so harrowing that at all times, a doctor
and clinical psychiatrist will be in attendance to
minister the faint-of-heart.

        THE CENCI, ladies and gentlemen, ripped
from the soul of Shelley, excavated from the
heart of Stendhal and transformed by the mind of
Antonin Artaud into the first and unforgettable
example of The Theatre of Cruelty.

        See the lovely and noble Iya Abdy as
Beatrice—suspended on a wheel of torture—by her
hair.

        See Antonin Artaud as the corrupt Italian
nobleman commit the most unspeakable
crime known to humanity.

        Hear sounds like you've never heard before. A
stereo-phonic tempest that splits the heavens.
The great bell of Amiens Cathedral reproduced
on four separate loudspeakers.

Get your tickets now, ladies and gentlemen,
for a theatrical work that will give an entirely
new meaning to the word tragedy.

*(Short drum roll and cymbal crash. ARTAUD
stands holding a sheaf of bills.)*

IYA ABDY: *(Discernible russian accent)* O M'sieur
Artaud, how can I thank you for this great chance.
Not only to act, but act one of the great tragic
figures of all times. Beatrice Cenci. Dark, brooding,
haunted daughter of a tyrannical father with
unnatural and profane desires.

ARTAUD: Lady Abdy, I am honored that a woman
of such a noble Russian family is prepared to
condescend to . . .

IYA: Not another word of that, M'sieur Artaud. I
am no longer Lady Abdy, but simply Iya. An
actress, an artist. Just like any other ingenue in
the bistros of Montparnasse. Now, I have been
working on this speech for Act Three. Tell me
your opinion, M'sieur Artaud, for I know that for
you the artistic temperament reaches heights
which can only be described as . . . *(She gestures)*
And anything you ask of me—anything! I shall
perform. Think of me as your Trilby. Mesmerize
me as you will! *(Begins to act)* "All is tainted.
All my body has been made a filthy thing, but
it is my soul that has become truly polluted.
There is no longer a single fragment of myself
in which I can take refuge. My crime . . . is to
have been born."

ARTAUD: Madame Abdy . . .

IYA: Iya.

ARTAUD: Madame Iya, the owner of the Folies
Wagram is anxious to receive a small advance
payment for the hire of his theatre. Not that he
has any misgivings about the reliability of our

        enterprise or the surety of your own celebrated
        ñame, but only because . . .

IYA: "Now I know how lunatics suffer. Madness is
        like death. I am dead, and yet my soul clings
        desperately to life and cannot free itself from
        its bonds. Ah, this savage world . . .

ARTAUD: Only a few thousand francs will calm
        his perturbed spirit, Madame. You see, he seems
        to believe that . . .

IYA: *(Suddenly studious)* In the scene just after Cenci
        has violated her, as she comes staggering from the
        bedroom of the hideous old man, I thought one
        should have a sound, a scream that would convey
        all the anguish of a daughter whose sex has been
        torn up by the root. Something like . . . *(Screams)*
        What do you think?

ARTAUD: Yes, there is something nicely primitive
        about that. However, before we decide on the
        finer points of the interpretation, could we
        address ourselves to the more immediate question
        of the advance, for I fear, without some small
        token payment, we may find that . . .

IYA: No, it's too banal.

ARTAUD: Madame?

IYA: Too diluted.

ARTAUD: Dilu . . . ?

IYA: Too much like the sounds that issue from the
        Comédie Française which, as you so rightly say,
        is only a lavatory for French culture. No, This
        scream must say it all. Everything that has been
        smouldering in Beatrice's tortured soul must
        find release in this one, supreme sound . . .
        (Screams)

ARTAUD: Perhaps if you were to have a word with
        him personally. I'm sure that alone would remove

any doubt concerning the solvency of our . . .

IYA: Or perhaps . . . *(Screams again)*

ARTAUD: You see, M'sieur Balthus also insists on a
small sum without which, I fear, the decorations
are in jeopardy, and without the requisite . . .

(IYA, *experimenting, screams again.)*

ARTAUD: . . . materials for the decor, it is difficult,
indeed impossible, to realize this project in the ideal
way that . . .

(IYA *screams again)*

ARTAUD: You and the entire company wish it to
be realized; that is to say, in a spirit of . . .

(IYA *screams again.*

ARTAUD *unable to take any more, screams
horifically and magnificently.)*

IYA: *(Pause. Awe-struck)* Yes, yes. That's it.

(SOUND *of* ARTAUD'S *cry of Tarahumara chant.*
ARTAUD *placed on stretcher by* DOCTORS.

ARTAUD'S VOICE *on* TAPE *in following scene.)*

FERDIERE: *(Lecturing)* Now as to the specific
issue of seismotherapy . . .

(ARTAUD'S VOICE *on tape. Scene as described
is played out behind* FERDIERE.)

ARTAUD: I died at Rodez under electroshock. I
say dead. Legally and medically dead.

FERDIERE: This has been torn entirely out of
context.

ARTAUD: The coma of electric shock lasts a
quarter of an hour. Another half hour and the
patient is breathing. But one hour after the
shock, I had not awakened, and had stopped
breathing.

36

FERDIERE: The electric shock produces an
             epileptic fit. After the convulsive stage, there
             follows a coma which may last several minutes,
             sometimes longer.

ARTAUD: Worried by my abnormal rigidity, an
             attendant had gone to get the physician in
             charge, who after examining me with a
             stethoscope, found no signs of life.

FERDIERE: There is always a short period of
             sleep—which is usually very short but difficult
             to determine, and finally there is an awakening.

ARTAUD: Since an hour and a half after shock, I
             had still not come round, Dr. Dequeker
             believed me to be dead. He sent for two
             asylum guards to remove my corpse to the
             morgue.

             (ARTAUD *examined, pronounced dead, about
             to be rolled away, suddenly sits up.*)

FERDIERE: On awakening, as in all epilepsies,
             there is a gap. The epileptic does not know what
             has happened. He asks, What am I doing here?
             Where am I? Who am I? This is absolutely
             normal.

ARTAUD: Personally, I have a different recollection
             of that incident. But I kept it to myself until I
             was able to confirm it later, with Dr. Dequeker.

FERDIERE: This kind of sub-anxiety on waking is
             on a psychopathological level a natural—even a
             desirable phenomenon. It forces the patient who
             has been reduced to nothingness, totally
             obliterated, to build himself up again. To follow
             the process of dissolution with the process of
             reconstruction—which is precisely what we are
             aiming at.

             *(Same scene now played out in slow motion,
             surrealist style. Menacing version of previous*

37

scene where DOCTORS *were kindly and sympathetic.)*

ARTAUD: And this recollection is that everything which Dr. Dequeker told me, I had seen—not from this side of the world but from the other.

FERDIERE: Convulsive therapy is a perfectly conventional form of treatment.

ARTAUD: Thus wrung out and twisted, fiber on fiber, I felt myself to be the hideous corridor of an impossible revulsion. And I cannot say what suspension of the void invaded me with its groping, blind spots, but I *was* that void, and *in* suspension.

FERDIERE: It is an entirely painless therapy. Of that one is absolutely certain.

(ARTAUD is carried from trolley and placed on stool beside DR. FERDIERE'S chair.

FERDIERE takes up "Alice In Wonderland".

ARTAUD takes up pad.

During next dialogue, ARTAUD'S excitement progressively increases till it reaches climax.)

FERDIERE: "What sort of people live about here," asked Alice.

ARTAUD: "Quelle sorte de gens habite par ici?"

FERDIERE: "In that direction," the Cat said, waving his right paw round, lives a hatter . . ."

ARTAUD: "De ce côtè-ci," répondit le Chat, remuant la patte droite, vit un Chapelier . . ."

FERDIERE: "And in that direction," waving the other paw, "lives a March Hare."

ARTAUD: "et de ce côté-là vit un Lièvre de Mars."

FERDIERE: "Visit either you like."

ARTAUD: "Visitez celui qui bon vous semble . . ."

FERDIERE: "They're both mad."

ARTAUD: "Tous deux sonts fous."

FERDIERE: "But I don't want to go among mad people," Alice remarked.

ARTAUD: "Mais je ne tiens pas à me'en aller chez des fous."

FERDIERE: "Oh, you can't help that," said the Cat. "We're all mad here."

ARTAUD: "Oh, vous n'y pouvez rien: nouse sommes tous fous par ici."

FERDIERE: "I'm mad. You're mad."

ARTAUD: "Je suis fou. Vous êtes folle."

FERDIERE: "How do you know I'm mad." said Alice.

ARTAUD: "Qu'ien savez-vous, si je suis folle?"

FERDIERE: "You must be," said the Cat . . .

ARTAUD: "Il faut bien que vous le soyez."

FERDIERE: "Or you wouldn't have come here."

ARTAUD: "Sinon vous ne seriez pas venue ici."

(ARTAUD rushes forward to VAN GOGH, standing with shaving-mug, open blade and mirror.

VAN GOGH lathering up ear. During dialogue, he prepares to sever it.)

ARTAUD: Vincent, you have been here before. You can help me. You are the only one who can. Before I arrived here, in that unreal world which was for me, the real world, I had a few—perhaps half-a-dozen certainties. Now I have none. None at all.

VAN GOGH: You should be glad. To be free of
certainties is to be free of lice.

ARTAUD: I need guidance, not epigrams, and *they*
are all of no use to me. But you, Vincent, you
are a full-fledged lunatic. Perhaps the greatest of
all the divine madmen. I could understand you.

VAN GOGH: What is a genuine lunatic, anyway?
I'll tell you. He's a man who prefers to go mad in
the social sense of the word rather than forfeit a
certain higher idea of human honour. The lunatic
is the man that society does not wish to hear; the
man that society wishes to prevent from uttering
certain unbearable truths. Internment is not the
only weapon, you known. Men have other ways
of undermining the wills of those it wants to
break.

ARTAUD: Dr. Ferdière has given me a book to
translate. ALICE IN WONDERLAND. He thinks
it will get me back on the rails again.

VAN GOGH: *(Stops lathering)* A book about the
hallucinations of a young English girl . . . ?

ARTAUD: He is the Chief Psychiatrist at Rodez.

VAN GOGH: Oh, I see.

ARTAUD: I think he is hatching a conspiracy against
me.

VAN GOGH: Please, I have enough delusions of my
own.

ARTAUD: Not against me. But against my double.
The part of me that threatens him; that would
try to change the world through my art.

VAN GOGH: The old trick. Dr. Gachet told me that
he wished to reform my painting—instead he
sent me to paint from nature, to bury myself in
a landscape to avoid the pain of thinking. But no
sooner had I turned my head than he cut all

contact with me. Not intending any harm or
ill-will, but simply turning up his nose as one
would at a harmless trifle. It is by just such a
gesture that the heedless bourgeois of the earth
have registered the old magic force of a thought
frustrated a hundred times. But Dr. Gachet liked
to leave the impression that he was my last
friend on earth, a sort of providential consoler.
Dear, good-hearted Dr. Gachet.

ARTAUD: I have been bewitched. A spell has been
cast upon me. Someone, somewhere is
siphoning off my health.

VAN GOGH: We are all bewitched, my friend. My
evil genie was Dr. Gachet, that slimy and petulent
Cerebus in sky-blue jacket and over-starched
linen who stood before me slowly stripping me
of all my sane ideas. There were any number of
putrid family confabulations between Theo and
Dr. Gachet and the directors of the asylum of
which I was the subject. "Make sure that he
entertains. No more of those ideas," "You see,
the doctor says no more of so-and-so, you must
dismiss all those ideas. They're doing you harm.
If you continue like that you'll be confined for
the rest of your life." "You were promised that
sum would be paid you. It will be paid. You
can't go on blaming the delay on ill-will." Those
are the kind of good-natured, psychiatrist's
conversations which seem to be perfectly harmless,
but they leave the trace of a small black tongue
in the heart, the small black anodyne of a
poisonous salamander. It was precisely after one
of these conversations with Dr. Gachet that I
went out into my fields as if nothing had
happened, and committed suicide.

ARTAUD: I spent nine years in an insane asylum
and never had any suicidal tendencies, but I
know that every conversation I had with a
psychiatrist during the morning visit made me

long to hang myself because I realized I could not slit his throat.

VAN GOGH: Bravo, bravo, Antonin. You have the makings of a first-class lunatic. A non-pareil.

ARTAUD: Do you really think so?

VAN GOGH: Without doubt, and just imagine the marvellous company you shall be in. Baudelaire, Rimbaud, Gérard de Nerval, Edgar Allen Poe. Anyone can become a great artist. All it takes is a firstclass PR man and a few well-placed newspaper articles, but to be a poète maudit, that is a distinction.

ARTAUD: *(After a pause)* May I show you some of my paintings?

VAN GOGH: Do you think I'm running a bloody gallery? Besides I am too busy organizing my posterity. I've a providential rendezvous with Kirk Douglas.

(Takes hold of ear and slices it off on Blackout.)

FERDIERE: *(Lecturing)* We were concerned then, and it is important to be clear on this point, with a madness that was, on the one hand, extremely fantastic, but which, on the other, preserved both intelligence and sensibility. To use the word *madness* does not, in psychiatric terms, mean "the impairment of intellectual powers." That is what people, uneducated people, cannot seem to grasp. Many patients wander in their minds, but often retain memory, reason and judgement— unimpaired. To be a madman and to be a great poet is by no means an irreconcilable antithesis. But I must remind you, immediately before our course of Electro Cardiograph Therapy, Artaud was by no means a great poet. He was, to all intents and purposes, only a madman. Afterwards, however . . . *(Crosses to* ARTAUD *who is in chair with sketchpad)* . . . as you can see, my friend,

42

things are beginning to look up. You've begun to
sketch again. Your letters are now two and three
pages long whereas before, you couldn't bear to
lift a pencil. Your translations are helping me
enormously. I cannot thank you enough for that.
And you are abandoning some of your more
fanciful ideas. Now you must agree, that is so.

ARTAUD: *(After a pause)* Dr. Ferdière . . . *(Pauses)*

FERDIERE: Do not hesitate my friend, speak your
mind.

ARTAUD: Is it true that schizophrenics sometimes
possess insights denied to normal minds?

FERDIERE: There is a school of thought that believes
that.

ARTAUD: And that is the disease from which I
suffer . . . ?

FERDIERE: It is merely a diagnostic label, my
friend. I wouldn't prey on it.

ARTAUD: I have had such an insight, doctor, It
has come to me several times.

FERDIERE: Good, good. Any kind of mental
activity that keeps away morbid thoughts is to
the good.

ARTAUD: May I speak of it.

FERDIERE: Of course you may.

ARTAUD: I have often felt, that after our morning
chats or our evening sessions, when my eye
unexpectedly caught yours, that you were looking
at me not like a doctor calculating doseage, but
like a mute acolyte, emitting a small, tremulous,
shiver of envy. That far beneath the endless
layers of starched-linen which is the inpenetrable
armour of your world, you wished, not so much
to cure me, but to seize for yourself, that
twisted, evil genie that made me a poet.

43

FERDIERE: *(After a pause)* It is quite common for you to have such feelings. You should feel no guilt about them.

ARTAUD: It is not guilt that I have begun to feel but ... violation. In my long, drugged sleep, I came to realize that unless I held firm to what it was you were trying to uproot, I would lose something far more precious than my sanity.

FERDIERE: In illnesses such as yours, a certain amount of paranoid delusion cannot help but ...

ARTAUD: Tell me, Doctor, for I know you are a kind man and have my welfare at heart, I do believe that: do you not at certain amounts in our meetings, or afterwards as you trudge into the sanctuary of your private apartments, do you not wish you could take away with you some of the inner-frenzy which has brought me here to Rodez?

FERDIERE: Thoughts of this kind, I can assure you, are entirely normal for someone at your stage of treatment. The main thing is not ...

ARTAUD: *(Slowly hotting up)* Confess, Doctor, for something of this truth has mixed itself with the fumes steaming from my charred brains ...

FERDIERE: You are exciting yourself, my friend, and that cannot help to ...

ARTAUD: Confess, that in that underground dungeon where you stoke your own darkest thoughts, you crave one flicker of that very conflagration you are trying to quell ...

FERDIERE: M'sieur Artaud, I had hoped we could talk calmly about matters which ...

ARTAUD: Confess it ... confess it.

FERDIERE: It is understandable that you should believe ...

ARTAUD: Confess it!

44

FERDIERE: ... that such fantasies should occur during ...

ARTAUD: CONFESS IT!

FERDIERE: *(After a beat)* IT'S TRUE! *(Eyes averted)* It is true.

(ARTAUD *approaches* FERDIERE, *his fingers outstretched and, without touching the* DOCTOR, *moves them trembling over the outline of his crestfallen form—as if tracing the contour of a magnetic field.*

Lights flicker. ARTAUD *disappears. New light cue leads immediately into next.*

BLIN *rushes in with revolver and* HENCHMEN, *takes* FERDIERE *prisoner.)*

BLIN: Tie him up. Here, put him in this.

(Straightjacket is put onto FERDIERE. BLIN *then goes to imaginary window.)*

Can you hear me out there?

DR. D: *(Off)* Yes, we can hear you.

BLIN: I have your precious Ferdière up here. I am training my revolver at his temple and unless the following demands are met, I will splatter his head against the wall.

DR. D: *(Off)* Are you all right, Gaston?

FERDIERE: *(Nonchalantly)* Yes, quite comfortable, thank you.

BLIN: First Demand: that the torture of Antonin Artaud cease as of the present moment. Second Demand: that Antonin Artaud is freed immediately and put into the custody of me and my friends. Third Demand: that declarations be signed by Ferdière and all the doctors in his employ, stating that Artaud is not, and never has been insane. That his incarceration and torture

has all been the fiendish plot of a bourgeois
nation that cannot tolerate the freedom of the
artist who sees through its cant and hypocrisy.

DR. D: *(Off)* Is that all?

BLIN: *(Defiant)* Yes, that's all.

FERDIERE: You'd better ask for a getaway car;
that's quite usual.

BLIN: Fourth Demand: a 1939 Citroën, three gallons
of petrol and an unimpeded journey through Paris
to Orly airport.

DR. D: *(Off)* M'sieur be reasonable. No one has ever
had an unimpeded journey from Paris to Orly.

FERDIERE: You might as well ask for a Rolls. You
do have the upper hand.

BLIN: Make that a Daimler and *six* gallons of petrol.
And anyone attempting to write a speeding-ticket
will be shot on sight.

DR. D: *(Off)* Is that all?

BLIN: *(Fiercely)* And two croissants and four carafes
of vin rouge, vintage 1919.

DR. D: *(Off)* May we discuss your demands.

BLIN: Certainly not. There shall be no compromise—
none whatsoever. Perhaps on the year of the
vin rouge, but that is all.

DR. D: And if we accede to these requests, what then?

BLIN: Then I shall only shoot your precious
Ferdière twice in the temple instead of six times in
the stomach.

DR. D: *(Off)* Could you possibly improve on that offer.

BLIN: Certainly not. I am not here to negotiate with
bourgeois pigs, but to free a poet, wrongfully
imprisoned.

DR. D.:   *(Off)* May I ask if you have seen M'sieur Artaud of late?

BLIN: How could anyone see him? He's been plunged into obscurity by your henchmen. Put into solitary confinement and tortured beyond human endurance.

DR. D: May I suggest you open the door immediately behind you and to the right.

BLIN: Do you think I'm going to fall for a childish trick like that? I've read my Raymond Chandler; seen all the Sam Spade films. Who do you think you're dealing with?

DR. D: *(Off)* I assure you, it's no trick. But if you would open the door to your right, it would greatly help to expedite matters.

BLIN: *(To* FERDIERE*)* You open it.

*(*FERDIERE *shrugs in straightjacket.* BLIN *grunts and stealthily approaches door, then flings it open.* ARTAUD *also in straightjacket, emerges.)*

BLIN: Antonin, it is I, Blin, your friend; come to liberate you.

*(*ARTAUD *looks long at* BLIN—*then at* FERDIERE—*then turns and begins to drone in a mechanical voice.)*

ARTAUD: *(In straitjacket; dull & monotoned)* There is an old story everyone is talking about, to themselves, but which no one will speak of in their everyday affairs despite the fact that it occurs publicly every minute of the day, and that, by a sort of nauseating general hypocrisy, no one will admit he has realized it, has seen it or lived it. This story is one of a spell cast over all, in which everyone more or less takes part, more one day and less the next, but all the while pretending not to know and wishing to hide from himself that he partakes in it, at times unconsciously, at other times subconsciously but more and more consciously.

47

The aim of these spells is to stop something I started
years ago, that is, to leave this stinking world
and have done with this stinking world. If I was
confined eight years ago and have been kept
confined for eight years, it is a result of a deliberate
decision of general ill will which desires, at any
price, to stop M'sieur Antonin Artaud realizing in
life the ideas he reveals in his books, because it is
known that M'sieur Antonin Artaud is endowed
with means of carrying out his ideas which they
desire to stop him using, when, with the help of
certain souls who love him, he wants to leave this
servile, idiotic society, asphyxiating both for
himself and for others who take pleasure in this
suffocation.

This is what I think, and what I think I am capable of doing, I already tried at Marseille in 1917,
during the last war, when all the tramps, the workers
and the pimps of Marseille followed me, and a taxi-
driver offered to chauffeur me for nothing, while a
man in the crowd slipped me a revolver to defend
myself against the police, and it is for provoking a
riot of this kind in Dublin that I was deported. But
this is no reason to make me out a madman, in
order to get rid of me, and to put me to sleep with
electric shock treatment so that my inner memory
is made to lose its energy.

(Turns directly to audience) All this is, of course,
personal, and does not interest you, I can tell,
because one reads the memoirs of dead poets, but
alive you wouldn't send them a cup of coffee or a
glass of opium to cheer them up. But if you listen
carefully to all I say, you will understand the fate
which middle-class France makes a rebel poet
undergo.

(BLIN *backs away incredulous and shattered, puts
down revolver and gives signal for* FERDIERE *to
be released. As* BLIN HENCHMEN *move off,* BEAT
POET *with long hair [beatnik stereo-type] cruises
out and begins to untie* ARTAUD.)

BEAT POET: Oh man, real cool. Right on, right on. You really know where it's at. I'm really knocked out by you. It just blows my mind, no shit.

ARTAUD: There is a value in cliches if they are comprehensive enough and do not ask to be taken at their face value but only as an acknowledged—accumulation of linguistic debris.

BEAT: Man that's beautiful. That's just what I think. Cause I been through all that scene. The Becks, Grotowsky, it really spaced me out. All that mainstream jazz and that Broadway shlock is nowhere. Hype-tripe, if you dig me. But that Cruelty caper is far out. The end, man.

ARTAUD: To be admired by thoroughly contemptible persons gives the career a certain fillip, but in the long run, tarnishes the reputation amongst those more refined intellects who recognize the distinctions between vulgar crowd-pleasing and aesthetic achievement.

BEAT: 14 carat gold, man. I was at Big Sur in '58 y'know. One night I got smashed with Ginsberg and Kerouac. Somebody laced the tequila with LSD and I thought it was just stale coke. Got into a little automatic writing out there. Got me this second-hand Webcor, and every morning I taped the first word that was spoken on the nine o'clock news. After three and a half years, I had a sonnet of fourteen lines that was so wild, I almost got interviewed by David Frost. I woulda stuck to that, but I wanted to get into audio-visuals and multimedia acid-rock with synthessor backings; that's when I met this chick that had found a copy of your book in an old church hall in Paris after Peter Brook and that mob had split to Afghanistan. It just turned my head right round. I knew—just like that—that I had to make the archetypal trip through Mexico via Dublin and get me some of those metaphysical goodies.

49

ARTAUD: Being a legend in one's lifetime provides certain monetary rewards which, sometimes greater artists, must do without, but dying alone and penniless after ten years of ferocious obscurity and mental torture is in no way compensated for by the vacant chunterings of the imbecilic young (and not-so-young) for whom the artistic life is on a par with Gene Kelly in sailor pants dancing down the mildewed steps of the Quai d'Orsay.

BEAT: Go man, go.

ARTAUD: And do me the like kindness.

(BEAT POET *takes hold of* ARTAUD's *hands.* ARTAUD *pulls away, leaving* BEAT POET *holding empty strait-jacket.*)

BEAT: Beautiful . . . beautiful . . .

(Lights out.

In darkness, ALL *take positions in semi-circle around* MME. MALAUSSENA)

MARIE-ANGE: I knew Antonin was lost as soon as his so-called friends swooped down upon him. At Rodez, he was attended to. When he asked for drugs, he was denied them. The sheets were clean; the floors were swept. In some small way, God was in attendance there.

FERDIERE: You are too kind.

MARIE-ANGE: To have a mad brother is not the most charming thing in the world. It doesn't make for refreshing conversation on the boulevards of Paris, and on Sunday, after church service, one knows it is only forced sympathy that makes people inquire after him.

ONE: How is old Tony? Still nutty as a fruitcake?

MARIE-ANGE: *(Politely)* Quite well, thank you.

TWO: Still using his magic shillelegh as a golf-stick?

50

MARIE-ANGE: No great change, actually.

THREE: Still bathing with his clothes on? Sucking
light-bulbs? Fucking doughnuts?

MARIE-ANGE: *(Politely)* Well looked after, I believe.
One was used to all of that. He was a deranged
child; a tortured adolescent, and an eccentric young
man. It only followed that he should become a
raving maniac. But when people insinuate he was
anti-Christ, they lie in their teeth. Although he
strayed when he was with his godless friends on the
left bank, he eventually returned to the faith.

ARTAUD: God has given me the strength to look into
myself and rid myself of evil.

MARIE-ANGE: Oh, Antonin, you've come back. *I
knew you would.*

ARTAUD: Sweet Jesu—I do renounce the devil of
sexuality and eroticism which fouled my mind and
infested my books. I disown "Le Theatre et Son
Double" and all diabolical influences that diverted
me from your gaze. In Christ's gospel and in the
Zohar which contains the word of the Father
himself there is a description of the world as it was
before Adam's fall, and one understands that it is
absolutely in no way God's fault, but Man's.

(Interjection as at Gospel meeting.)

ARTAUD: And that Man only became miserable and
rejected when he had betrayed the original and
angelic conception of things by weakening to
sexuality.

(Interjection.)

Jesus Christ did not say, Go forth and multiply.
He said Go forth and multiply like the angels.

(Interjection.)

Only in that way can we arrive at a state that will
gladden God's heart.

(Interjection.)

Every time a sexual act is performed something is
spoilt in the universal life.

(Interjection.)

When we commit erotic acts, we blot out the
Heavenly light.

(Interjection.)

But I have found that light.

(Interjection.)

Here. At Rodez.

(Interjection.)

In the love that surrounds me, in the warmth of my
friends.

(Interjection.)

In Gaston Ferdière.

(ALL *hot-Gospel it, led by* MARIE-ANGE.
FERDIERE *gives communion to* ARTAUD *up-stage
while* ALL *cavort around them.*)

ALL: Jesus loves me, this I know,
For the Bible tells me so,
Little ones to him belong,
They are weak, but He is strong.

Jesus loves me, He who died,
Heaven's gate to open wide,
He will wash away my sin,
Let His little child come in.

FERDIERE: *(Lecturing)* You see, there are many
people who only came to know Artaud after his
death, and it is from these people, in the main, that
the Artaud myth has sprung up. "He was a tortured
poet. Very misunderstood. People were unkind to
him. He had a terrible life." And of course, in the
construction of this myth, it must follow that he

52

was as normal as you or I. Not at all mad. And also
necessary to the myth is the villain; the sadist, a
kind of Doctor Caligari with a more or less diabolical
face. And this is the role into which I have been cast.

(LIGHTS UP *on* ARTAUD *tied to stake with
cigarette drooping from his mouth.*)

MARIE-ANGE: Never, Doctor Ferdière. You were his
saviour. But . . . how could you bring yourself to . . .
who could have persuaded you to . . .

BLIN: Turn him into a phantom; an empty shell.

DOCTOR: Is this the noble poet whom our French
Academy called all-in-all sufficient.

BLIN: The man who could have alchemized the
French theatre.

DOCTOR: Is this the nature whom passions could so
shake?

MARIE-ANGE: To throw him from his sanctuary,
that was a sin.

BLIN: To brainwash his poetry . . .

ONE: To hook him on drugs . . .

TWO: To pull out his teeth . . .

THREE: To use him as a guinea-pig . . .

MARIE-ANGE: To claim he was godless . . .

(ALL *bear down on* FERDIERE *repeating their
lines. He suddenly stops them, draws out a scalpel
and holds them at bay.*)

FERDIERE: Soft you; a word or two before you go.
          I have done the state some service, and
               they know it
          No more of that.—I pray you, in your
               letters,
          When you shall these unlucky deeds relate,
          Speak of me as I am; nothing extenuate,

Nor set down aught in malice. Then must
    you speak
Of one that lov'd not wisely, but too well.

Of one not easily jealous, but being
    wrought
Perplex'd in the extreme; of one whose
    hand
Like the base Judean, threw a pearl away
Richer than all his tribe; of one whose
    subdu'd eyes,

Albeit unused to the melting mood,
Drop tears as fast as the Arabian trees
Their medicinal gum. Set you down this:
And say besides:

I am a man more sinned against, than
    sinning.

*(ARTAUD escaping oncoming CROWD.
Jumps from stake)*

ARTAUD: *(Suddenly recalling)* I've just remembered.
It all happened before. It was a play, in the twenties,
one of my first roles.

*(DULLIN appears with script as before. A door-flat
is placed on stage.)*

DULLIN: *(Directing)* All right . . . get ready . . .
positions. Everyone in position. Artaud, further
back, behind the door. You're still visible from the
front. Further back, further. Good. Ready. Ready
at the door, and begin!

(Points to ARTAUD, giving a cue.)

ARTAUD: *(Off stage)* May I come in?

(Door opens.)

DULLIN: . . . and BLACKOUT.

(Lights out.)

and Curtain! *(In darkness)* Good. We'll have a short

break and begin from the top after lunch. Bon
appetit.

(All leave in dark.

Lights go up on solitary ARTAUD.

On tape, ARTAUD's *voice repeats;* "May I come
in?" *sepulchrally.*

ARTAUD *standing in spot,* MUSE *appears.)*

ARTAUD: Am I to blame? Is it my fault?

MUSE: *(Pityingly)* Oh, Antoine.

ARTAUD: *(Disconsolately correcting)* Antonin.

MUSE: Sorry. You got only what you asked for.

(ARTAUD *moves disconsolately upstage-centre
and sits on stool.)*

ARTAUD: I never asked for this. I wanted success—
like all the others. I went on my knees to Jouvet,
to Dullin who had taught me, to Barrault, whom
I practically invented. Not even the sweat from
their balls. None of them.

MUSE: You chose, Antonin. You chose for yourself.

ARTAUD: Choose, what did I choose?

MUSE: The far-table at the Deux Magots, the secluded
corner at the Café Flore. The black cape, the
crushed hat, the shillelagh of St. Patrick.

ARTAUD: That *was* the shillelagh of St. Patrick. I had
divine and irrefutable proof.

MUSE: *(Patronizingly)* Of course you did. You chose
to be the tourist attraction. You could have had
success. It was always within your grasp.

ARTAUD: *(Wearily)* Lies, lies, on every side.
Everywhere I turned they shat upon me.

MUSE: You gloried in it. Anguished, misunderstood,
the makings of legend.

ARTAUD: I would have traded it all for a bungalow
            in Antibes.

MUSE: Not for you, Antonin. The easy success; the
            four-page spread in Paris Match. The other road
            for you; the gravel path.

ARTAUD: *(Trying to muster contempt)* I was *in* the
            tradition, you pewling cow, don't you realize that?
            Villon, Jarry, Baudelaire, Artaud. We offered
            society a chance to purge itself. We rammed in the
            suppositories to clot its bleeding piles. We burned
            like buddhist monks, the crackle of our new
            perceptions lit up in the dark wastes of France.

MUSE: *(Patronizing)* Of course it did.

ARTAUD: And now, I am expected to lay down like
            a soggy corn-flake drowned in milk. *(To* MUSE)
            You know I was a true visionary. Admit it.

MUSE: Of course you were, but France doesn't need
            visionaries. Really Antonin. How could you be so
            penetrating about other things and not realize you
            were in a land where everyone wears thick spectacles
            and walks with a white cane.

ARTAUD: If I had been given the chance . . .

MUSE: *(Admiringly)* What wonders you would have
            achieved.

ARTAUD: That's true, isn't it.

MUSE: That will always be said about you, Antonin.
            Isn't it satisfying to know that in centuries past you
            will always be given the benefit of the doubt.

ARTAUD: *(Philosophically)* Yes, that is some
            consolation. And yet . . .

MUSE: Yes?

ARTAUD: I keep going over all the events to try to
            find where I went wrong . . .

(In following scene as each character appears he or she is holding the empty cut-out of a mirror in which their own faces are framed. During scene they very slightly preen themselves while speaking.)

MARIE-ANGE: When you turned your back on God, and the family, you were lost.

ARTAUD: *(Wearily)* You priest-ridden cow. You need God up the arse; a great flaming shaft of Him corruscating your prostrate gland and choking you with His holy sperm.

MARIE-ANGE: Father wanted you to have everything. You were always the favourite. You turned your back on it all. Grave error.

ARTAUD: How can anyone abide Christ when he keeps such abominable company.

FERDIERE: He could never shake off his God. He railed at Him all his life. Christ was a bone stuck in his throat.

ARTAUD: You tried to raise Christ in your Frankenstein laboratory. Electrocute him back to life.

JOUVET: *(With pity)* Artaud le Momo.

RIVIERE: He added a certain colour to the scene. France depends on its lunatic fringe—just as England does on its eccentrics.

ARTAUD: I opened my heart to you, and all you did was to make me into a literary event.

RIVIERE: If he'd only have known where to stop, he could have made the French Academy. We've taken worse.

BLIN: You should have annihilated them all, Antonin.

ARTAUD: My fine friends, always eager to shoot me from their cannons to show their support.

BLIN: We idolized you.

57

ARTAUD: Worship, but never sympathy.

MARIE-ANGE: God could have given you that.

ARTAUD: He waited long enough.

DR. D: He unconsciously clamoured for rejection.

ARTAUD: The Freudian quarter heard from.

JOUVET: He had a certain talent. That was undeniable.

BLIN: Then why did you spurn him?

JOUVET: "Spurn" is a word out of Victor Hugo.

ARTAUD: No one ever fish-fried his brains.

MUSE: No, but hippies never visit his grave.

ARTAUD: How nice to truly rest in peace.

BLIN: *(To* JOUVET) You were frightened of him. Admit it.

JOUVET: He used to carry a knife, you know. Not a stage knife where the blade sank into the handle, but a knife with a cutting-edge that could draw blood.

BLIN: *(Sarcastically)* You were frightened of his knife?

JOUVET: I only mention it in passing.

FERDIERE: What was it then? I was always curious myself.

BLIN: Why did you slam the door in his face?

JOUVET: One simply wasn't at home when he called. That's something quite different.

ARTAUD: Too busy touching up Molière.

ALL: The deader the artist, the greater the love.

> (ALL *put down hand mirrors and turn to* JOUVET.)

58

JOUVET: Whatever you think of me and my generation, we were custodians of a tradition that went back four centruies. To be such a custodian is a serious business. It means securing culture against the pirates and the sneak thieves that would pilfer its riches. I would never join the military if my country were invaded. I would declare my neutrality and sit things out till the smoke had cleared. But if anyone threatens my tradition, the succession of cultural events that nourishes and gives my life meaning, to safeguard that, I would fight to the death.

At base, Artaud was an enemy to culture; a marauder. A man whose sensibility constantly threatened our own, and so he had to be isolated. Just as the victim of the plague, his dear, wildly-theorized plague, was isolated. Unemployment is a useful form of isolation, but not certain. Incarceration, that is foolproof.

All honour to Dr. Ferdière and Rodez. At a time when all the hallowed traditions of France were being threatened by the onslaught of anarchy and annihilation, and one of its most deadly carriers was within the walls of the city, he contained the plague.

ARTAUD: *(To* MUSE) If I come again, as I believe sometimes happens in the endless course of time, could you possibly manage Maurice Chevalier or Fernandel. I'd be most obliged.

(BLIN, *banked on every side with* SUPPORTERS, *bursts through and confronts* FERDIERE *with a petition.)*

BLIN: We, the undersigned, demand the release of our friend and compatriot, M'sieur Antonin Artaud, who, for almost ten years, has been the prisoner of the French medical establishment which has methodically destroyed the sensibility of one of the greatest French artists to emerge in this century. In the words of Artaud himself, We protest vigorously agains the right attributed to certain men, narrow-minded

59

TWO: or supposedly open-minded,

THREE: to sanction with sentences of life-
    imprisonment

FOUR: their investigations into the domain of the
    human spirit.

ONE: And what imprisonment!

TWO: We all know,

THREE: no, we do not know well enough.

FOUR: that asylums

ONE: far from being asylums,

TWO: are fearful jails,

THREE: where the inmates provide a source of free
    and useful manpower,

FOUR: where brutality is the rule,

ONE: all of which you tolerate. A mental hospital.

TWO: under the cover of science and justice,

THREE: is comparable to

FOUR: a barracks,

ONE: a prison,

THREE: a slave-colony.

FOUR: We protest against any interference

ONE: with the free development of delirium.

TWO: It is as legitimate,

THREE: as logical,

FOUR: as any other sequence of human ideas or acts.
    Madman are,

ONE: above all else,

TWO: the individual victims of social dictatorship.

THREE: In the name of that quality of individuality

FOUR: which belongs specifically to Man,

ONE: we demand the liberation of these people

TWO: convicted of sensibility.

THREE: For we tell you that no laws are powerful enough

FOUR: to lock up all men

ONE: who think

TWO: and act.

BLIN: Try to remember *that* tomorrow morning during your tour of inspection when, without knowing their language, you attempt to converse with those people over whom you have one single advantage:

ALL: Force!

BLIN: Signed: Robert Desnos, André Gide, Arthur Adamov, Jean-Louis Barrault . . .

FERDIERE: Gaston Ferdière.

BLIN: Eh?

FERDIERE: I agree.

BLIN: What?

FERDIERE: I agree—he should be released. And may I remind you, it was your own Robert Desnos who pleaded with me to accept him in the first place. However, after extended treatment, both medical and psychological, I feel the time has come to restore Artaud to society.

BLIN: *(Incredulous)* You mean he's cured?

FERDIERE: Cases like Artaud can never be cured; let's be clear about that. One can teach him how to behave properly with other people. One can dissuade him from seizing the throat of young women whose clothes displease him. One can bring him to that point of social stability where it is

61

possible for him to sit at a table, use a knife and fork, chat idly and while away the time. And one can, one *has*, restored the writer to his metier. At Rodez, he has written what André Breton believes to be his masterpiece: Van Gogh, The Man Suicided By Society. He has composed a variety of curious, somewhat delirious letters which nevertheless, must be counted as an important part of his output. I do not wish to exaggerate his accomplishment nor my own. My task has been to make a man fit for society, thankfully, without asking whether society is fit for him. This I have done.

(As BLIN *and* OTHERS *stride out,* MADAME MALAUSSENA *strides in and over to* FERDIERE.)

MARIE-ANGE: *(With hand-out)* Are you going to permit this to take place?

FERDIERE: My dear Madame Malausséna, it has nothing to do with me.

MARIE-ANGE: Because of you my brother has been released; because of you he will now be made the laughing-stock of Paris.

FERDIERE: Come, come, Madame.

MARIE-ANGE: *(Reading from Handout)* 'The Return of Artaud le Momo." Do you see? "Artaud le Momo"—Artaud the Madman. In print, for all to see.

FERDIERE: It is your brother who insisted on that title.

MARIE-ANGE: My brother is a sick man, and now, thanks to his so-called friends, a drug-addict to boot. But even that is not enough for them. Now, they must parade him like a music-hall monkey for all to mock.

FERDIERE: Madame, your brother needs rest and quiet in a private nursing home. That costs money. This benefit will raise close to one million francs.

62

His security will be assured. Is that not worth one night of his life?

MARIE-ANGE: To be ridiculed—to display one's illness at a side-show!

FERDIERE: You seem to forget Artaud has been absent from Paris for almost a decade. Divorced from his friends and his society. This is a first, tentative, step towards that society. The audience at the Sarah Bernhardt will be made up of writers and poets . . .

MARIE-ANGE: Gapers, sensation-seekers . . .

FERDIERE: His friends from years ago. In a sense, one can regard this evening as part of his post-Rodez therapy.

MARIE-ANGE: You must forbid it.

FERDIERE: I have no authority.

MARIE-ANGE: It will kill him. He is not ready for anything like this. He should be protected from such things.

FERDIERE: In cases like this, the patient is often the best judge of his needs.

MARIE-ANGE: I shall never forgive you.

FERDIERE: *(Getting exasperated)* Madame.

MARIE-ANGE: It is you, doctor, who is throwing him to the jackals.

FERDIERE: According to his friends, it is I that am the Jackal.

MARIE-ANGE: If you permit this scandal . . .

FERDIERE: M'sieur Artaud is now a free man. He has been petitioned out of Rodez and into the custody of his friends. Since that release, I have been abused, maligned in the press, and on the stage of the Sorbonne, spat in the face. I refuse to

be dragged into posterity on the apron-strings of
Antonin Artaud. My job is finished. I am through
with him.

*(Corny intro-music as for TV Variety Show. MC in
sequined jacket arrives.)*

MC: Ladies and gentlemen, Messieurs et mesdames, at
great expense to the management of le Théatre
Sarah Bernhardt, we are proud to bring you, direct
from a record-breaking run at some of the finest
mental asylums in France . . . The Clinic of Chazal
Benoit, The Hospital of Ville-Evrard, the world-
renowned Rodez . . . a man who really needs no
introduction.

Some of you may remember him from his
notable filmic appearances in such classics as
"Napoleon", "The Wandering Jew", "The Wooden
Cross", "The Passion of Jeanne d'Arc", of his own
record-breaking and unreleased "The Seashell and
The Clergyman".

Yes, ladies and gentlemen, tonight we bring you
a man who, though in his late forties, is now on the
first rungs of a terrific comeback. *(Becoming over-
earnest)* A man who, for the past ten years, has
been waging a terrific struggle against the dread
disease of mental unhealth, and who finally, after a
lot of love and electrical assistance, has almost got
it licked.

Now I know we all want to get on with the show
and I don't want to take time away from this
famous artist who has taken great pains to be with
us here tonight.

(Digresses) And it warms my heart—I've got to
say this—to see an audience filled with such
marvellous celebrities as André Gide, Albert
Camus, M'sieur Pablo Picasso—all pulling for our
boy to make good.

Ladies and gentlemen, messieurs et mesdames,
by courtesy of Dr. Gaston Ferdière, The French
Electricity Board, and all the boys at Rodez who
made this appearance possible, I give you—the one
and only—Antonin Artaud.

(MC *gestures to centre spot.* ARTAUD *now dressed in conventional grey suit with shirt and tie, slowly moves forward into spot. He is holding a sheaf of papers, his address. From behind him all the* MEMBERS OF THE COMPANY *slowly appear holding a double mask on a stick. Each face on the double mask depicts a slightly unreal staring face with white staring eyes.*

ARTAUD *begins to fumble with his notes. They flutter out of his hands. He tries vainly to assemble them. The more he tries, the more they tumble out of his grasp. Eventually they all fall and lie scattered about him.* ARTAUD *stands motionless. The* ACTORS *holding the staring masks slowly turn them around revealing the reverse-side which contains a wry, cruel smile.*

A coffin is ceremoniously brought on stage, SEVERAL MEMBERS OF THE COMPANY *move affectionately over to* ARTAUD, *lift him into their arms and gently place him in the coffin; he, dazed and disbelieving.*

MARIE-ANGE *and the* MUSE *ceremoniously place the lid on the coffin, then step back into a semi-circle.*

ALL *clasp their hands in front of them and bow their heads for a moment of prayer, then slowly move off in various directions.*

From the coffin, the barely audible sound of banging can be heard. ALL THE MOURNERS *stop in their tracks and slowly turn towards the coffin. The banging inside the coffin gradually increases in volume. The* MOURNERS *look uneasily from one to the other, then after a moment's hesitation, continue to walk off, leaving only* DR. FERDIERE *and* ROGER BLIN *who stand regarding each other uncertainly. Then* FERDIERE *turns and leaves.* BLIN *hesitates for another moment and also turns and goes.*

The coffin now spotlit remains isolated and alone in the centre of the stage. The banging inside it increases in volume until it becomes unbearable. SLOW BLACKOUT.

APPENDICES

The following conversations were transcribed in 1966 while preparing a radio-broadcast on Artaud for the BBC. They are heavily edited. Roger Blin, (born 1907) one of Artaud's earliest protegés, is today one of France's leading directors. His productions include the premières of Samuel Beckett's WAITING FOR GODOT, ENDGAME, KRAPP'S LAST TAPE and HAPPY DAYS. He has also directed the first productions of Jean Genet's THE BLACKS and THE SCREENS. Arthur Adamov (1908-1970) was, with Beckett and Ionesco, counted as one of the leading Absurdist writers of the 50s and one who strongly revealed signs of Artaud's tutelage. In his later work, the Brechtian influence became more prominent. His works include L'INVASION, LA GRANDE ET LA PETITE MANOEUVRE, PROFESSOR TARANNE, PING PONG, and PAOLO PAOLI. The two articles THE ANTONIN ARTAUD AFFAIR: WHAT SHOULD BE KNOWN by Marie-Ange Malausséna (Artaud's sister) and I LOOKED AFTER ANTONIN ARTAUD by Dr. Gaston Ferdière, chief psychiatrist at Rodez, originally appeared in the TOUR DE FEU of December 1959 and are reprinted here by courtesy of that magazine.

MAROWITZ: Can you give me an account of your first meeting with Artaud?

FERDIERE: I am going to speak chiefly about my first meeting of Antonin Artaud at Rodez, but I knew this personality, Antonin Artaud, a long time before that. Because at that time, I moved in the same circles as Artaud, the post-Surrealist, para-Surrealist circles, if you like. And during this period, my friends often asked me to take him in hand. They told me his behaviour had become increasingly outrageous; that he was more and more given to fits of anger; that he behaved odiously in society, and at times, with an incoherence that made them fear the worst.

In particular, as you may know, Artaud had, and was never separated from a walking stick, the stick of St. Patrick, and with this stick he used to threaten harmless customers sitting outside the literary café, La Coupole. I refused to take Artaud in hand because I myself was entirely devoted to what you might call, if you like, poetic liberty and, besides, I think that my interference would have been absolutely useless. It only proved useful in 1942, and why? What was happening at that time? Well, the mental patients of the psychiatric French hospitals were threatened with death because it was the height of the Occupation and the food restrictions were such that starvation became almost inevitable, which led to a general debility and eventually to the grave. Artaud was one of these patients, and at this time, he was interned at the mental hospital at Ville Evrard. He was what they call insane, a madman who had become completely withdrawn from society—even unable to eat, which was curious because Artaud was a big eater, as I learned afterward. Here, he had become very thin and he was totally inactive. I emphasize this because very soon we shall come back to these problems of the activity and behaviour of Artaud. In any case, one of his dearest friends, a mutual friend, the poet Robert Desnos, one day warned me of the situation and said "I beg you, we can't possibly stay aloof any longer. We must save Antonin Artaud."

We all agreed with Desnos that Artaud should be brought

across the dividing line between life and death. I was able to guarantee that he would receive, in my own psychiatric hosptial at Rodez, of which I was the director, the good care which was due him. Desnos was not only the most delightful of friends and the most devoted, he also knew a great many people. He went to the police headquarters of the Seine, made many manoeuvers and eventually, we succeeded in getting Antonin Artaud across the line of demarcation. First of all, we got him to a branch psychiatric hospital of the Seine, a place in the Seine that is always disposing of its excess mental patients (because in Paris, you know, we always have too many psychopaths and we can't wait to be rid of them.) It was a hospital of which I had formerly been the director. It was agreed that my colleague would keep Artaud for a few days and then transfer him immediately afterwards to Rodez. So Artaud left Paris. He went briefly to the psychiatric hospital of Chezal-Benoit, and then one morning, accompanied by a nurse, arrived at Rodez.

It was 6 o'clock, 7 o'clock, 5 o'clock in the morning—I don't remember exactly. I went to meet him at the station. I saw Artaud get out of the carriage and come towards me vigorously expressing his thanks. He greeted me as if I were an old friend, a friend whom he had been seeing regularly. Let me be very exact here. I had often seen him at a distance but I had never been close to him. I couldn't tell him he was making a mistake. I realized his mind was wandering. I realized, too, that he was threatened by an extremely grave mental illness. For this reason, I immediately answered *yes* to whatever he said. "You remember when we were at such-and-such café? When we were in Montparnasse on such-and-such a day?" I said, "Yes, certainly I remember. It's nice that you've come here." And before long, I was treating Artaud no longer as a sick man withdrawn from the world, but as one treats an intimate friend. And I tried from that moment on to restore the human quality that he had lost. My wife helped me to play my little game which, after all, was in the nature of an experiment and so, when we arrived at Rodez, she immediately invited him to lunch. To say there was anything pleasant about that lunch would be to tell a lie. It was something that had to be got through for love of Artaud, and poetry, simply for love of Antonin Artaud and poetry. And there, in those surroundings, my wife displayed an absolutely admirable patience. She herself is a psychiatrist.

She thanked Artaud for coming to lunch with us. She put up with all his improprieties—they were numerous during the course of the meal—he had probably not eaten in public or seen a table-cloth for years. She put up with all his dirty and disgusting eating habits. She put up with him chanting and kneeling down between courses, etc., etc. It was after all this bad behaviour at meals that we decided, after a few days, to give him a private room. To do this in a provincial psychiatric hospital in France was far from easy. After only a few weeks in the asylum—("Asylum" because these psychiatric French provincial hospitals retained the characteristics and habits of the former lunatic asylums) in the *asylum* then, Artaud had his private room in which he could do practically as he liked and which, I must say he kept in a horribly dirty state. From time to time, we had to clean it; to remove the remains of old food or tobacco which lay about everywhere. There was even a certain drama in getting him, once a week, to the bath and the showers. (You know, even in his early years the actors who worked with him were often horrified by his bad smell.) At certain times, he practically gave up washing, and I had to insist before he came round to obey me (I excuse myself for using this word *obey*) and would consent to go with the nurses to the bathroom. And so you see, it was only at that time that I took Artaud in hand. Long before his friends had begged me to look after him. It was necessary to have absolute control to try to save the life of this man, and I must say, that under these terms, I agreed to intervene.

MAROWITZ: But as to the specific nature of his madness?

FERDIERE: This idea of madness is one that leads us all into error. Under the law of 1838, an ancient law by which in France we classify madness, people who are dangerous are certified. Now Artaud had been, and always was, in the truest sense, a dangerous man; a man society should eliminate; from whom society had a duty to protect itself. He had been—you remember—placed in psychiatric hospitals following an incident which had occurred on the ferry that brought him back from Ireland. He went to Ireland to retrace the footsteps of St. Patrick as, a few years before, he had gone to Mexico in search of ancient Indian rituals. And on the boat that brought him back from Dublin, he had an attack of violence which forced the captain of the vessel—the sole master of his craft after God—to put him in a cell in the hold of the ship to protect the other passengers from harm. On arriving at Le Havre, Artaud was taken off the boat and taken immediately—I think bound in a straightjacket—to the hospital at Le Havre. Soon afterwards, they transferred him to the psychiatric hospital at Rouen. Unhappily the records at Le Havre and Rouen were burnt during the Liberation of France and in spite of all my efforts, I have not one document from this period except the orders for internment.

MAROWITZ: But as to his illness . . .

FERDIERE: Yes, we're coming to that. I saw a man who had emerged from his withdrawn state, who was not eminently dangerous at that moment, but who, in his attacks of madness, could be. If you would like me to summarize this insanity in a strict psychiatric way, I would say this: In the madness of Artaud, there was a kind of combat, a gigantic combat, a manichean combat, between God and the Devil. And it was sometimes God who triumphed and made of Artaud a man possessed with a burning faith, going several times a week to Mass, spending hours with the almoner of the hospital, and at other times, a person praying to the Devil, who insulted passing women and spat on imaginary people. And it is for this reason that I cannot, as François Mauriac does in France, make a great mystic of Artaud. I would have to make him a great mystic and a great madman in the same breath. We were concerned here with a madness that was extremely fantastic but with a notable preservation of intelligence and sensibility. To use the word *madness* does not in psychiatry mean "the impairment of intellectual powers". This is what people, uneducated people, do not readily understand. There are people who wander continually in their mind, but who retain memory, reason and judgement unimpaired. This conflict between God and the Devil is the current coin of the Trappists. We find it at all mental levels. We also find it among people who are completely uncultured as, for example, the shepherds in our mountains, as well as in people who are extremely cultivated who, in Paris, for example, move in intellectual circles or in universities. It is one of the commonest manifestations of psychopathy. What I don't want to give here, apropos of Artaud, is a diagnosis because the present-day psychiatrist is wary of diagnoses. To diagnose mental illness, to say one thing is given this name and another thing

70

another name, is a very great danger because one cannot class the mentally sick as one classifies insects, butterflies, or flowers. It is necessary that in each mentally sick person we should, above all, see beyond diagnoses and labels, to the human being. Now as for the human being that was Artaud, what was the matter with him from the point of view of mental illness? Was he a schizophrenic? Well, yes, in a certain sense he was, but schizophrenia is a veritable cancer which has devoured all our patients, especially those who are touched with hallucinations, among the schizophrenics. For Artaud I would, on the contrary, prefer to put an accent on that intellectual preservation of powers which we had still to prove was in existence because, as I have told you, there was no sign of it at the beginning, and so I would prefer to employ an old word from German psychiatry and say that he was a *paraphrenic*.

MAROWITZ: And how did you progress with your patient?

FERDIERE: Well, here is Artaud at Rodez. He finds himself in the most sympathetic surroundings we have been able to procure for him. He has a private room, as I already told you. He has enough to eat, even, I might say, an abundance. L'Aveyron is a rich province and a province where there was a good black market. And the director of a psychiatric hospital, as I then was, fed his patients by means of the black market. So Artaud is well fed. Artaud is a heavy smoker and so he smokes, because the same director also dispenses the packets of cigarettes and tobacco that Artaud requires. And he gives him as much as he asks for. Artaud is surrounded by people who visit him in his room. There is a painter for instance, Frederick de Langlabe who, at this time, is an escaped prisoner who has taken refuge in my apartment and who never lets a day go by without visiting him or going for a walk with him through the grounds of the psychiatric hospital. For Artaud now begins to go out. He even goes beyond what are called the living quarters and soon he ventures outside the gates of the hospital. First in the company of a trusted friend, and then entirely alone.

What treatment does he receive? First a treatment that I would call physical; to be well fed is an important part of any treatment. He takes a number of tranquillizers, he does not have drugs. (I will come in a moment, to the question of the possible drug poisoning of Antonin Artaud). And yet Artaud always remains in a kind of stagnation, in a kind of inactivity which is deeply disturbing. Here we are dealing with one of the greatest poets of his generation. We are dealing with the man who wrote *Le Théâtre et Son Double,* who was going to revolutionize the contemporary theatre, and here he sits doing nothing, sunk in hidden thoughts. One day, he must be brought out of this and it is for this reason I consider myself authorized to get something moving, to prevent Artaud from sinking hopelessly into insanity—because now it *is* insanity that lies in wait—intellectual weakening this time. I decided to use seismotherapy and Artaud received a number of electric shocks which, it must be admitted, he remembered with horror and if you like, we will speak of how Artaud faced these shocks and I will rell you the truth.

MAROWITZ: How many electric shocks was he given?

FERDIERE: I think it must have been about nine times—six to nine times. About that—if I remember what was customary then, because medical custom varies from year to year.

MAROWITZ: These electric shocks, they must have been extremely experimental at this stage? Very little was known about electric shocks in the mid-forties.

FERDIERE: It was perfectly well known. It's a convulsive therapy, and before electric shock treatment was used, we gave patients other forms of shock-treatment which were perfectly well understood and which were widely used. Instead of producing a kind of epileptic fit through electricity, we administered drugs intravenously, drugs which are called cardisol and I even remember having given patients cardisol in 1940. So we already have convulsive therapy, a classic treatment in the hands of a psychiatrist, and the experimental stage had long since passed. In the psychiatric hospital at Rodez, we dealt with about a dozen electric shock cases a day.

MAROWITZ: Artaud said that after one of the electric shock treatments he was actually dead for about five minutes. Is that true?

FERDIERE: Yes, of course, because the electric shock produces an epileptic fit. After an epileptic fit which develops stage by stage, the convulsion stage succeeding the period of stimulation, a coma follows which may last several minutes, even sometimes a little longer. Then a period of sleep, which is very short, finally

72

an awakening. But on waking, as in all epilepsy, there is a gap. The epileptic doesn't know what has happened. The epileptic who has a fit in the street asks the people standing round him: "Where am I?" Well, Artaud asked the patients around him, the nurses, the passing doctors, "What am I doing here? Where am I? Who am I?" That is absolutely normal, and this kind of sub-anxiety on waking is, on the psychopathological level, a healthy phenomenon. It forces the patient who has been reduced to nothingness, who has been totally obliterated, to build himself up again and to follow the process of disollution with the process of reconstruction—which is precisely what we are aiming at. So you see, Artaud had suffered no more nor less than the other people. From the electric shocks, he felt absolutely nothing. Electric shock is an entirely painless therapy, of that we are absolutely certain. What is difficult is rediscovering oneself, finding oneself back again in the world after the electric shock. I could compare it, if you like, to the kind of disorientation you experience when you wake in a strange bedroom, in a hotel room for example, where the light does not strike your eyes in the same way as in a room to which you are accustomed. That's what it's like. Nothing more. And in spite of all that Artaud has said about the horrible electric shocks, the barbarous therapeutic electric shocks, it is by this same electric shock treatment that he was able once more to realize where he was.

MAROWITZ: And after these electric shock treatments, was Artaud much changed?

FERDIERE: It was then that Artaud asked to read again. We let him read. We gave him everything we could get in wartime. He read all the books that I myself received. He read *Alice in Wonderland* because I thought it important to try and get him back into writing by means of translation and so I used this pretext of helping me, saying to him, "I know very little English and if I translate it, I shall make many mistakes and misinterpretations. Help make an adaptation of *Alice* for me." And he did an adaptation of *Alice*. I also gave him a text of which I am very fond, Southwell's, *The Burning Babe* and he made a translation of this for me. This translation I then sent to Pierre Seghers and it appeared in an edition of his magazine, Poetry. And, it was the first time Artaud was published since his internment. We could therefore once more begin to indulge in some very real hope for him.

MAROWITZ: Did you know that Artaud was suffering from cancer when he came to Rodez?

FERDIERE: Artaud never had cancer when I knew him. Artaud's cancer is one of the myths that encumber Artaud's life. Perhaps in the last days he suffered from an acute form of cancer which carried him off, but until further evidence comes up, I refuse to believe there was cancer in Antonin Artaud at Rodez. He never showed the least sign of cancer, certainly no intestinal or abdominal cancer which is what is in question here. These can easily be detected and are rapid killers. Artaud died very much later without having had a single symptom of cancer.

MAROWITZ: Now so many years afterward, has your impression of Artaud and his treatment altered in your mind?

FERDIERE: Anyone who saw him regularly, who lived with him and saw him develop, sensed this mental sickness in him a long time before his voyage to Ireland. One knew very well, one day or another, it was going to explode. If it had not blown up on the boat that brought him back from Ireland, it would have happened somewhere else. One fine day after a brawl, they would have taken him to some police station and shut him in a padded cell or to the special infirmary at the Paris police head-quarters. We all knew very well that it could only end in that way.

MAROWITZ: And what do you say to Artaud's friends who claim Artaud was not actually mad?

FERDIERE: It's an opinion of those who never saw Artaud, who never knew him. Just show me that man whether he's an engineer or a teacher or a poet or whatever you like, who knew Artaud, who saw him living in Paris well before his internment, and who will contend that Artaud did not behave like a tremendously unbalanced person. Those who say he was not mad are his friends who saw him in his last days; those who became the 'Friends of Artaud' after his death. An Artaud myth has grown up and in this myth it is said: he was a very great poet, he was very isolated, very set apart and people had attitutudes to him which were very uncharitable, almost inhuman. And, in the construction of this myth it has to be said: he was a normal being, he was not at all mad, and one puts in opposition to this, another person also necessary to the myth: the psychiatrist, the villain, the sadist who makes his patients suffer, a kind of Doctor Caligari with a more or less diabolical face—and this is the role into which I have been cast.

MAROWITZ: Were you in Paris during Artaud's last days?

FERDIERE: No, I was not in Paris at that time. You are probably referring to the lecture he gave at the Vieux Columbier.

MAROWITZ: Yes.

FERDIERE   I was myself not there at this lecture. But my friends who were there were horrified; horrified to see Artaud put on a show in a really terrible state—prey to every sort of delirium and excitement, gesticulating, shrieking, spitting, vituperating—not able to get his words in the right order or read the lecture he had prepared. But what made them even more sick at heart were those who looked on, who had come there just to gape, to *watch* the show, with an all-too-apparent smugness. And I know too there were many people who came out of love for Artaud, saying "Artaud is speaking tonight, we must go." But who came out of the theatre that evening absolutely sickened by the attitude of the audience around them.

MAROWITZ: Then you would say, after his period at Rodez he was not cured.

FERDIERE: Artaud could never be cured. He had a mental illness that was incurable. What does curing a madness like Artaud's amount to? Simply this: to make it possible for him to live in society. Artaud when he left Rodez was a gentleman who had learned how to behave properly; that is to say, without seizing by the throat the first man that he met or insulting a passing woman because she was wearing a blouse which displeased him. That is all the cure that was ever possible.

CONVERSATION WITH ROGER BLIN

MAROWITZ: Can you remember the first meeting with Artaud?

BLIN: It was at a film club—sometime in 1928. It was during that time when he was having one of his reconciliations with the surrealists. He had just finished filming in Dreyer's *The Passion of Jeanne d'Arc* and he still had his hair tonsured like a monk. That's to say, the top of his head was entirely shaven and the rest of his hair was about a centimeter long. And this is the way he used to go about Paris. We were all booing an American film, I remember, and it was at this moment that I first encountered Artaud. He wanted very much to adopt me as his son—I don't really know why—and afterwards we met very often in Montparnasse at the Coupole, and spent many evenings together with friends. I helped him with his work, Heliogabolos, and afterwards with a variety of notes that were later to become the basis of *The New Revelations of Being.* I used to go to his Theatre Alfred Jarry. I remember especially the production of *Victor ou les Enfants ou Pouvoir,* and one day Artaud said to me after a performance of this play: "Would you like to be my assistant? I have a plan to mount *The Cenci*—I've made an adaptation based on Stendhal and Shelley—would you like to work with me?" I of course agreed, and we went in search of a theatre. It was difficult. We had very little money, but we finally found a place which we weren't mad about but was perhaps acceptable, a former music hall in the Avenue de Wagram, and we started rehearsals in a small adjoining room.

Artaud used to hold a large notebook in his lap and have some coloured crayons nearby—one colour for each member of the cast—and he used to say to me: "Make a note of everything I say" and opposite the text I had to draw diagrams of the movements which he indicated for each character. And then, one day, he said to me "Make notes on everything I say, make *careful* notes on what I say and even on what I *don't* say. You must act as a medium and be able to perceive what I think and what I'm going to say."

He wanted the actors in the banquet scene of *The Cenci* to act in a stylized manner. He wanted each of the princes to resemble an animal. But it was extremely difficult, because none of the actors had any idea whatsoever about this kind of acting. They had not been trained in this way at all. They came from the Conservatoire or commercial theatres where all that was asked of them was good diction. Artaud also asked them to make certain throaty noises—which they found very difficult. One day, after we had searched in vain to find two or three actors to play the deaf-mute assassins, he asked me to go onto the stage. This was something about which I had no idea whatsoever, but he

76

found that I wasn't too bad and that is how I came to act for the first time in my life—in *The Cenci*.

MAROWITZ: Did these actors understand Artaud's ideas?

BLIN: Most of the actors understood Artaud's ideas but carried them out rather badly because Artaud had not taken the trouble to fully explain his meaning. He was completely wrapped up in his subject and he had faith, perhaps too much faith, in their abilities immediately to comprehend his intentions. Perhaps we needed more time for rehearsal—especially to find parallels—to find certain simple images to help the actors understand because, I must say, it all appeared a little abstract to them. Nevertheless it was the true, the great theatre that Artaud wished to introduce them to.

Artaud was always searching for some kind of basic truth, and having come up against an almost total lack of comprehension in France, he thought he would find in Mexico a country, a language, a people (the Indians) who would be much nearer to him, nearer to his innermost self, and who might understand what he wanted to do. And so he journeyed into Mexico.

MAROWITZ: Would you say, in your meaning of the word, that he was a 'revolutionary?'

BLIN: That would be difficult to say. It was precisely on this point that Artaud had a terrible clash with the surrealists who at that time were following the Communist Party line. He himself was not anti-Communist. But he looked further, much further, and quite clearly he had no class sense. In fact he was at once terribly human and terribly aristocratic. And when *he* spoke of Communism he was thinking of the royal Communism of the Incas or the Indian civilizations. So obviously there were areas of great misunderstanding.

MAROWITZ: During the mid-Thirties at the time of *The Cenci*, what did the Parisian world think?

BLIN: They were not very impressed. As for *The Cenci*, the critics came. They found that it was not too bad, some even found it fairly interesting. But it was just one more item on the balance sheet of the avant-garde. Perhaps it reached certain young people in the auditorium and for them, it has remained a tremendous memory. But in Parisian life, during the fifteen to seventeen days of its production, it passed like the wind. It absolutely failed to make any mark.

77

MAROWITZ: What sort of man was he?

BLIN: I never knew so fascinating a man, a man so generous
and capable of such kindness and understanding of others.
Perhaps he was difficult to live with because of a kind of separa-
tion that he tried to establish between himself and others, and
also because of the agony he suffered in the face of the almost
total incomprehension that surrounded him. I can't speak for
anyone else, but for me he was the most fascinating man I ever
met.

MAROWITZ: It would appear that he made many enemies in
Paris.

BLIN: It was not so much that he had enemies. He had no
enemies; people were simply indifferent to him.

BLIN: It was before his departure for Mexico and then later I
saw him for a few days before he left for Ireland and then we
simply didn't know what became of him. There was some reports
that he was dead. He himself, it appeared, was responsible for
this rumour and then we learnt he was at the Hospital of Henri
Roussel at St. Anne. As soon as I discovered this, I went to see
him but he then didn't want to see me anymore—nor did he want
to have any contact at all with any of his former friends. He
didn't want to see anyone. He would only accept cigarettes. And
I remember I saw him in the courtyard of the asylum with his
back against a tree, wearing an enormous beard, and from time to
time I would come down to find out how he was. Afterwards, I
saw him at the asylum at Ville-Evrard where he had been sent by
the doctors who claimed his case was hopeless: that is, he was
absolutely finished, that he might have good health, but would
never recover his reason—that reason which I, for my part, never
believed he had lost. I went to visit him as often as I could and
eventually, he agreed to see his friends again until the time he was
sent to Rodez. Then of course under the Occupation, it was very
much more difficult to get through the various zones. We were
all living in a state of utter wretchedness in Paris, still, we did
what we could.

MAROWITZ: How did Artaud manage to get released from Rodez?

BLIN: There were a group of friends who managed to get Artaud
out of Rodez by organizing a variety of benefits. The Gallery
Pierre had organized an exhibition of his paintings, helped by

Picasso, Braque, and others who appreciated Artaud; and there was also a charity performance at the Sarah Bernhardt Theatre in which I took part. This was during this period that Artaud returned to Paris. But he was extremely ill. He already had the cancer from which he was to die eighteen months later. And it was at this time that Artaud and I saw each other more or less every day.

MAROWITZ: Had he changed greatly after Rodez?

BLIN: He was extremely changed—physically. That is to say , suddenly he was a man of only fifty who looked seventy, because of hunger, because of cancer, because of the electric shocks he had undergone.

A few months before his death, Artaud wanted to resume contact with his public—the only public he ever really knew—and so he announced a lecture at the Théâtre du Vieux Colombier which was to be called THE RETURN OF ARTAUD THE MOMO. "Le momo" is a slang word from Marseille which means the Madman. Of course it was a facetious title because he realized that is what he had been called, although he himself, of course, never truly accepted the label. He had very carefully written and prepared his lecture and to be honest, we were all rather apprehensive for him. Still, no one could dissuade him from delivering it. People have said, and also have written, that we egged him on to do it. Absolutely not! We simply didn't want to prevent him from doing it because he seemed so determined.

Well, in any case, to describe the occasion: Artaud enters and finds himself in front of a full house among whom were Albert Camus, André Gide, a great many people, many of them celebrated and all waiting with enormous curiosity. Many with genuine interest and sympathy but many more with naked curiosity. Slowly he assembles his material and he begins to read. For a long time, at the start, his voice was uncertain. He had some very deep bass notes and very high ones and because of his lack of teeth, because of the damage wrought by electro-shock therapy, he no longer had any middle range. It was an extraordinary voice and some recordings of it still exist. He began reading rather solemnly. Then little by little we could see that he became seized with panic. He began to hear his own voice and it frightened him. The full hall, the total and somewhat strained silence of the public, made him feel very ill at ease. Suddenly he made a clumsy gesture and all at once, his notes scattered all over the floor. He tried to pick them up; he tried to improvise. Then, seized with panic and terror, he turned from the platform and fled from the building. Afterwards we found him round the back. But it was a devastating affair, an absolutely shattering evening.

MAROWITZ: Do you think that a Theatre of Cruelty as described by Artaud is a real possibility?

BLIN: I really don't know. Having known him intimately I would say that it is possible to carry on his work to a certain extent—but it is really something which belonged very much to him. I don't believe one can use Artaud as an authority for a revival of this kind of theatre; not simply from the point of view of the theatre or from the point of view of a new aesthetic. No one can cite Artaud as their authority unless they have conducted a struggle similar to that which Artaud conducted on behalf of the body against thought and against God. It is not simply a matter of adopting outward mani-festations: breathing, mime, gesture, diction, cruel subjects. It's not a matter of simply using these things and then claiming one is following Artaud's footsteps. One cannot cite Artaud as one's authority unless one conducts a similar struggle against the idea of the soul, against the abominable fate nature has preserved for the body of man. This is why I cannot cite Artaud as *my* authority. One would have to have gone through the same kind of struggle against magic that characterized Artaud's entire life.

MAROWITZ: What importance do you think Artaud has had in the contemporary theatre?

BLIN: I'm inclined to think that fundamentally, Artaud's importance in the theatre means less than his importance on a philosophic level, defining a certain mode of thought.

MAROWITZ: Do you see Artaud's influence anywhere?

BLIN: I don't really see it because in so many cases where people acknowledge the influence of Artaud, they are dealing only in externals. One can discern the influence of Artaud centered uniquely on an aesthetic point-of-view—*that* one can see. A large number of people tend to quote him as their authority, as the American Beatniks did in the Fifties, but in a spirit totally alien from his own and with a total lack of understanding.

MAROWITZ: In a work like *Marat/Sade* by Peter Weiss, do you not perceive some kind of Artaudian influence?

BLIN: Not in the ideology of the play. Artaud for instance, would have loathed Charlotte Corday.

MAROWITZ: And what of the work of Grotowsky?

BLIN: Yes, I have heard of it. I have seen pictures of it. But there, too, it seems purely a matter of externals. Certainly very valuable research but essentially only the exterior ideas of Artaud.

MAROWITZ: Artaud railed against psychology and naturalism but do you see the modern theatre moving away from these things?

BLIN: For my part, I don't see it at present but I don't really know. After my work with Artaud, I had the good fortune to meet Samuel Beckett and Jean Genet who are very far removed from Artaud. Genet I think is probably nearer to Artaud than Beckett. I am sure, for instance, that Artaud would have hated *Waiting for Godot*, being a work of tragic resignation, because Artaud himself was profoundly optimistic.

MAROWITZ: Can you remember the last time you saw Artaud?

BLIN: The last time I saw him he was in a café. It was while he was waiting for the results of a meeting that had just taken place. The directors of the French radio had banned his broadcast "Pour Finir avec le Judgement de Dieu" which had been heard by a certain number of selected people who had now gathered together to protest against the ban. I had gone to the café to ask Artaud how the meeting had gone. We had arranged to meet the following day but the pressure of work had prevented me from doing so. And then the next day, Paule Thevenin rang me and told me that Artaud had been found dead that morning. I went immediately to Ivry to his room, and there I saw him. A few friends had already gathered there and so had his family, his mother, and his sister. We kept vigil over the body for three nights. We kept vigil in relays—although none of us were very keen on this ceremony, this watch over the dead, but we felt we had to do it because of the rats. For a

81

long time Artaud had been at odds with his family on the matter of religion. And so we kept watch against the rats at night, and against the priests who threatened to visit him by day. But they never came. Then, on the day of his funeral—the family of course had certain rights—he was buried. There were two sets of mourners: his family and his friends. Some people went to shake hands with the family, but not many, and, as he had wished, there was no religious ceremony. But it was really an occasion of immense sadness.

CONVERSATION WITH ARTHUR ADAMOV

MAROWITZ: Can you recall the first time you met Artaud?

ADAMOV: I can't tell exactly what day it was, but I do remember I was very young and it was in Montparnasse. It was at the time he frequented the Café du Dome and I used to meet him often there with my friend Roger Blin; it was also the time when Giacometti used to be found there and lots of other people. It was the heroic epoch of Montparnasse. Just about the time of the Wall Street crash. It was when the Dome was fashionable—full of young Norwegian and Swedish and English girls. It was the era of Blin and Giacometti shortly after the era of Modigliani, Lenin, and Trotsky.

MAROWITZ: And what was Artaud like?

ADAMOV: Artaud was always Artaud. In spite of all his illness, he always retained an extraordinary sense of humour; one of the people with whom you laughed most. Let me give an example of Artaud's humour.

He had a small knife, and in the clinic where we put him after Rodez in the care of Dr. Delmas, he used to amuse himself by carving on the table. Now Dr. Delmas didn't bother about someone carving up his table. He was a very nice man. But then, in the cafés, Artaud used to do the same thing. And one day a friend of ours, Marcel Buziaux who published a great deal of Artaud's last writings, said to him, "Now listen, Antonin Artaud, it's very boring of you really, because if you do this kind of thing in the cafés, they will send you back again; they'll say you're not right in the head." Artaud, who was very much like Buster Keaton, very deadpan, turned to him,

"But look my dear Marcel Buziaux, I only do it at the Flore and the Deux Magots." In other words, only in the cafés where he was known. Artaud was like that. You *thought* you were going to have trouble with him . . .

One day I remember, at the home of Marthe Robert who was a great friend, we were having a discussion and Artaud began to exasperate us by insisting that there were lamas in Tibet who were willing his death. I don't quite know why, but we were very irritable that evening. We couldn't really believe that he was mad and so we said, "Listen, Artaud, there may well be people who want you dead, but don't tell us they're in Tibet! Don't go on any more about Tibet," we said to him. And then he was very angry and left in a huff. After he'd gone I said to Marthe Robert, "We've really been stupid. We shouldn't have contradicted him like that. You see how angry we made him." Two days later, in the Rue Jacob, I came across Artaud, who suddenly burst out laughing and said "You remember that other evening at Marthe Robert's house? There's never been such good talk this side of a Dostoyevsky novel." And that was what Artaud was like. He had an immense and unpredictable sense of humour and the best way to pay homage to Artaud (and it is Blin who has said this) is not to say how sad everything was for him but to laugh uproariously as one recalls the way he used to laugh at almost everything. I think we love people to the degree that we can laugh when we remember them.

MAROWITZ: But after Rodez in Paris, he was terribly unhappy, wasn't he?

ADAMOV: No. On the contrary. It was the one time he actually had some money. It's the family who say he was miserable because the family never even sent him a ration card. Oh, yes, during the Fascist occupation, they sent him one bread card. It's a reactionary Catholic family, rich and disgusting, and they're always bringing lawsuits against Artaud's friends of whom I am proud to be one. And it's this family that prevents Artaud's most interesting works from being published. Although we sometimes get works from Gallimard that are interesting, such as Le Théâtre et Son Double that everybody is familiar with, or a few minor things, the family is still opposed to the publication of the great works of Artaud. So we have to spend time fighting our lawsuits. We have a lawyer and they have a lawyer . . .*

MAROWITZ: Has Artaud influenced your own writing?

ADAMOV: Not in a direct sense, indirectly yes. Artaud was himself influenced by Strindberg's *A Dream Play* which I once saw acted by him in an extraordinary comic manner and he was also deeply impressed by Büchner's *Woyzeck* and, as I have been influenced both by Strindberg and Büchner, I came to Artaud. But as I say, it was not a direct influence.

MAROWITZ: Do you see Artaud's influence anywhere in France?

ADAMOV: I, who love Artaud so much; I, who believe he was one of the greatest poets of the twentieth century, must admit that what is terrible about Artaud is the people who try to imitate him. Mostly, they are very poor specimens, intellectually feeble, who try by imitation to create a metaphysics far beyond their reach. And they are people who have not even read *Le Livre des Morts Tibetains, Les Poupés Javanaises* or *Les Restes du Surréalisme.*

MAROWITZ: Do you believe Artaud was mad?

ADAMOV: What is a normal man? What is a mad man? It was Jaspers who said "The majority of people are mentally defective". Now if one claimed that the normal man is representative of the majority, that would mean to say that the normal man is mentally defective. Not a mad-man, a mental defective. And, without taking up a ridiculously superior attitude, I would say that Jaspers is right. I don't know what is mad or not mad. I know there are people for whom life is very terrible, and what moves me most when I think of Antonin Artaud, what makes him one of the human beings I most love, is that in the middle of an immense poem, I don't remember the title, in the middle of this immense poem, a remarkable work, packed with brilliant images, he suddenly gives some words to the mother of his doctor, Madame

* The complete works of Antonin Autaud have in the meantime been published by Gallimard, Paris, in 12 volumes. See bibliography of English translations verso of title page of this volume.

Dequeker and she speaks this very simple sentence; "And old Madame Dequeker said, 'How difficult, comma, (it is I who put the comma) how difficult, how very difficult, how very difficult it is to live." I am grateful to Antonin Artaud because he always spoke of the difficulty, because he had endured it personally. He did not speak only of its absurdity like Monsieur Camus and the other existentialist small fry, no, because Artaud realized the point was not that life was absurd but that it was difficult.

MAROWITZ: Did you see Artaud in the last days of his life.

ADAMOV: Unhappily, I did. He was at the end of his tether. He had invented a fable for himself about being the victim of lamas in Tibet. And when they gave him permission to have all the morphine he wanted he understood very well that he was finished. You know that he took drugs all his life. It wasn't a secret to anybody. He suffered terribly. It was obviously cancer and not merely drug addiction as the family contended. The family always wanted to blame everything on drugs. No, on the contrary, the drugs in the last stages helped him to put up with the sufferings produced by cancer—and when one has a Catholic family . . . well, let's say no more of that.

MAROWITZ: What were the general impressions in Paris at the death of Artaud?

ADAMOV: Feelings were very mixed. It's difficult to say. There were people for whom Artaud truly represented the essence of poetry, and there were other people, the small fry, the hangers-on, who had made a false image of Artaud. It's very complicated to explain. There is a sort of caricature of Artaud which I personally find disagreeable, that makes him very much more insane than he was. In this caricature there is a kind of romantic madness which is played up. Although Artaud was in many senses completely rational . . . but to talk about Artaud properly would take years.

When I think of him, I think back to his Theatre of Cruelty plays for example, I think of one particular play that was produced during this period; a play with incredible humour . . . I want to talk about something that seemed absolutely astonishing to me in Artaud's life. It's what

85

he called the Theatre of Cruelty and remember when I was young (I was very young then, about sixteen), I remember being present at two performances of his Theatre Alfred Jarry. At one of these he had mounted the first act of a play by Paul Claudel, "Le Partage du Midi", and the first act of this play is quite good. Afterward, unfortunately, and here I am in agreement with Artaud, the play falls off—but the first act was good. (I should say, for those who know the play, that it's the scene on the ship.) Artaud had directed the play and as he very much enjoyed provoking people, he said at the end in a very mournful voice: "The play you have just seen was written by a great poet who is also a spiritual traitor." Paul Claudel, you see, was also a French ambassador. Before that, all the surrealists had been heckling and making little jokes. Some shouted "Vitrac!"; others shouted "Tzara!" And then, in the second part of the evening, they were showing a very good film of Pudovkin's called "The Mother" adapted from Gorki, and in this film there was this woman marching around endlessly with this red flag (this was well before the revolution). In these entertainments of Artaud's something extraordinary always happened, and on this occasion, all of a sudden from the depths of the orchestra-pit of the Theatre des Champs Elysées, a woman who was neither pretty nor ugly, old nor young, but marvellously well-dressed and loaded down with jewelry, began marching down the aisle while on the screen Gorki's mother marched around waving this red flag. The woman marched from the orchestra pit to the first row of the stalls shouting in English—she was an American—"Wake up, wake up to the Soviet threat!" The entire auditorium burst out laughing and it was an extraordinary explosive kind of laughter.

Another time Artaud wanted to put on Strindberg's *The Dream Play* but he had no money, and so he approached the Swedish ambassador and eventually he raised some. The Swedes haven't got very many celebrated writers, but they have got Strindberg and I suppose they thought it would be good publicity for Sweden. Artaud, at this time, was still a surrealist and André Breton, who was not always very bright, admonished Artaud saying "Are you really putting on a play by this nitwit, this dreary Strindberg?And are you also in favour of a Franco-Swedish alliance?" Artaud was very frightened of the surrealists and so before the play began, to try to excuse himself, he announced the same stage direction that Alfred Jarry had used at the beginning of *Ubu Roi.* You remember, in *Ubu,* it says "The scene is set in Poland; that is to say nowhere in particular." Well, Artaud repeated this sentence saying "This play takes place in Sweden; that is to say, nowhere in particular."—In order to pacify the surrealists who had said it was scandalous to take money from a foreign legation.

Well, at just this moment, (I'm telling you about the humourous side of Artaud because when you speak to people about him they always give you tragic stories, that's why I want to stress this other side) when he said "The action takes place in Sweden, that is to say nowhere in particular" an enormous Swede got to his feet and demanded that all Swedes should leave the theatre and he stomped out followed by a dozen other Swedes. Then, all of a sudden, a very small man— he wasn't quite a dwarf but he *was* very small—got up and said that the Danes should follow the example of the Swedes and he stomped out—but not one Dane followed him. This produced an immense outburst of laughter. Meanwhile, on the stage, Artaud holding an enormous bouquet of flowers continued to play his role of the officer in the opera-box shouting, "Mademoiselle Victoria." Mademoiselle Victoria replied from the wings, "I'm coming, I'm coming," but of course she never came. And at the same time, these petty surrealists—it was the surrealist epoch you know—had spied Paul Valéry in one of the boxes. He was with a very pretty woman, and they began to shout "Merde pour Valéry! Merde pour Valéry!" And then suddenly another surrealist, I forget who it was, cried out during this remarkable performance, "Down with France! Down with Sweden!" Then others began hollering "Up the Soviets! Up the Soviets!" Somebody else shouted "Long live Lenin!" Another yelled "Long live Trotsky!" Then, an old man slowly got to his feet, a very very old man, and he called out in a very frail voice, "Long live Charles Péguy. Long live France." Then there were about forty students shouting in the back "Down with France! Down with France!" And during the whole of this time, Artaud went on acting *The Dream Play* calling "Mademoiselle Victoria, Mademoiselle Victoria." It was completely mad, you know. You can't

87

possibly imagine the atmosphere that existed in the Theatre Alfred Jarry. It's gone forever.

MAROWITZ: What was the public reaction to Artaud's production?

ADAMOV: Well, it differed widely. There were some marvellous ideas in *The Cenci* for instance. Artaud wanted to empty the stage completely and then make it live again in a totally different way, but he had no money, he had no actors—well, there was an American dilettante who gave him some money—but no one knew how to act, it was all very badly done, marvellous ideas badly carried out. It was a very different kind of theatre. It had nothing to do with the crass stupidities of today nor the perfection and intelligence of Brecht's Berliner Ensemble. It was something quite different. Much more spontaneous. I've always found it pitiful when people try to imitate Artaud. There are certain people one should never imitate, such as Artaud and Van Gogh. These are people one must not imitate, then there are people, like Cézanne, whom we must imitate. But you know, in general, all those who speak to me of Artaud only see in Artaud exactly that part of him that seems unimportant to me, a kind of picturesque oriental side of Artaud which I have no time for, and is precisely the part of him which used to annoy me.

MAROWITZ: And the poetry?

ADAMOV: He was one of the greatest of all the poets. For me, there are three French poets of the twentieth centruy. I will tell you who they are: Apollinaire, Eluard and Artaud.

THE ANTONIN ARTAUD AFFAIR
WHAT SHOULD BE KNOWN

by Marie-Ange Malausséna
translated by Charles Marowitz

This affair is usually treated as an extremely complicated
one, in which the family does not exactly play an illustrious
role. But no-one really knows what it consists of, or why there
is an Antonin Artaud 'affair.'

But then how could you find your way through all this
claptrap of absurdity, ineptitude, contradiction, lying,
offensiveness and defamation which is its basis, or through all
the cheating and intrigue which are its results?

It would have no importance to me if my brother's memory
had not been damaged. Now it must be said that the picture
many people have of Antonin Artaud today is a false one.

In fact this 'affair' is very simple: the very day of Antonin's
death a great conspiracy was mounted against his family with
the sole aim of intimidation, for criminal acts had been
committed. His room had been thoroughly looted. Everything
he possessed—manuscripts, notes, drawings, books, correspon-
dance—everything had disappeared before we got there . . . for
they had taken care only to notify us 9 hours later.

Since then, certain people, trying to derive profit from their
theft, have managed, with some deviousness, to get themselves
in everywhere, and everywhere we have had to intervene.

So there are now more than twenty (legal) actions in
progress.

That's all there is to the Antonin Artaud affair.

I want to stand back from my own grief, but I want the public to learn the truth at last. It is with this aim in mind that I offer *my evidence, for which I take full responsibility.* The documents I produce are of unquestionable authenticity and mostly unpublished. Principally they relate to the following points:—

a. The defamation I have suffered; this continues because of rumours that I am opposed to the appearance of the 2nd volume of the Complete Works, when in fact, for the memory of my brother, *I am very anxious for it to come out. (I have no idea why* Gallimard are delaying publication of this volume. They should really think about changing their monogram to a sphinx's head!)

b. The indiscretion of certain out-and-out climbers who, by awarding themselves the title of friends of the poet, have made the expression "friends of Artaud" a pejorative one. How can one distinguish between his false and true friends? Of his real, sincere friends, one figure stands out and that is Mme. Toulouse, wife of the distinguished psychiatrist, who took an affectionate interest in him from 1920 on.

c. The false picture of Antonin Artaud as living apart from his family. Dr. Ferdière is responsible for a good part of this fiction by behaving as he did to my mother. I cannot keep silent about his strange behaviour to us.

That is why I make public the 3 letters which come at the end of my exposé, not so much to refute the idiots who echo absurdities as the result of a psycho-physiological auto-experiment. Everyone knows that he took drugs and it has been said that he had the heroism to go through with his mental self-destruction.

The truth is quite different. Certainly less melodramatic, but more pitiable in the real meaning of the word.

Antonin Artaud was ill all his life. He suffered the onset of meningitis as a small child. His nerves tortured him all his life. As no therapeutic drug could cure him, the doctors used sedatives; narcotics, in fact. There is no question of vice in his case. Nor of heroism. We should simply be quiet and keep silent.

But as legend has made of him a bloodless and fleshless being, having only a brash proclivity towards dementia, one must re-establish the truth and show just how extraordinary a human being my brother was. These letters are the proof. When I had defeated my slanderers, I became silent. If I break that silence today, it is because I decided that the Tour de Feu, impartial with no vested interests, was the only magazine worthy of enjoying my confidence and of supporting the truth.

*   *   *

Antonin Artaud did not like to talk about his family to just anyone. You had to be close to him.

So you must realize that those who say he didn't want to have anything to do with his family weren't close to him.

Well, it is exactly these people who boast now, and since his death, that they knew him well. They don't just boast of it, they proclaim it.

How well one understands them! . . .

For how else could they explain the fact—the well-established fact—that they are in possession of all the manuscripts, all the notebooks, all the correspondence. All the books and all the drawings of Antonin Artaud?

So to have been the friend, the counsellor, the confidant; to possess everything which belonged to the 'doomed poet' to be able to give published material to whoever asks—what an ideal springboard to fame!

But it would have been better still if the poet had had no family.

Certainly, but the fact is he definitely did!

So, the mother becomes an abusive mother, as do the brother and especially the sister. All three become abusive for having existed beforehand, and for still existing.

So there were two solutions; either the family would wash its hands of the whole affair, or you had to make the family disappear.

At first they tried to get round us. But Tartuffe made a mistake. He got in up to his neck.

Then they tried the heavy brigade. They loosed the secret weapon: slander. A defamatory campaign was begun secretly. And as a newspaper was indispensable for the battle, they chose the newspapers "Combat".

It began with a sharp and extremely hurtful attack. A

91

whole page of the newspaper was devoted to it with, in pride of place, a 4-column article in which libel and slander jockeyed for prominence. In this way, for weeks on end, they accomplished innumerable feats. His 'friends' at the end recklessly used everything which could sully, everything which stinks, everything which can kill, to get at the poet's family. They were successful. She whom the poet had loved so, his mother, died. She couldn't withstand such attacks.

This first result did not disarm anyone. On the contrary, they renewed the attack; but with less success. Things were actually going badly, so badly that:

By a judgement rendered in the 3rd Chamber of the Civil Tribunal of the Seine district, dated 2 March 1955, the journal "Combat" and the author of the article were found guilty of defamation against Mme Marie Artaud, wife of M. Malausséna.

I cannot pass over the notorious manifesto which followed the libellous article and was signed by 170 people. Here is the full text, published on 27 February 1950:

"A recent note in Le Figaro Litteraire *announced the creation of a Society of the Friends of Antonin Artaud, founded by Mme Malauséna, the poet's sister at the request of the friends of Antonin Artaud."*

Those who have the right to call themselves the friends of Artaud formed a society in May 1946—a society with an extremely precise goal: get Artaud out of the Rodez asylum and give him a chance to live.

At that time, the friends of Artaud received no help or support of any kind from this family. So they had to act as if that family did not exist.

Therefore they cannot admit that, under the pretext of protecting a work of which, by its own admission, the family has but the remotest knowledge, the family should make use of the name of that society.

Artaud's work does not need to be protected, it defends itself. It is in the process of being published, under contracts signed by the late poet. The only difficulties which have arisen so far have been caused by his family. Therefore it is inadmissable that the family should not content itself with drawing the royalties protected by law, but should also attempt to oversee a literary work which Antonin Artaud never shared with them.

So one can only consider as totally unjustified any opposition to the publication of Artaud's work coming from people who, although they are entitled to the profits of this publication— impatiently awaited by one and all and prepared by the poet's designates—can under no circumstances delay it.

This manifesto says: the friends of Antonin Artaud have had neither help nor support of any kind from the poet's family.

But it does not say: that at no time did they ever address themselves to that family.

It says: they had to act as if that family did not exist—At last, something true, quiet well-expressed, for them. *It goes on to say:* the friends got together to get Antonin Artaud out of Rodez asylum.

But it does not say: it was in order to put him in the Asylum at Ivry.

And it adds this manifesto: . . . and give him a chance to live.

But it does not say **how** *he would live!*

Jean Desternes in Le Figaro Litteraire, 13 March, 1948 says *"I go to see, for the first and last time, Antonin Artaud four days before his death, alone, in a bare room, at the end of the garden. He apologises for the wretchedness of his room, his tired hand indicates that hideous, peeling walls, the damp patches, the desolation around his bed which occupies the middle of the room."*

Jean Boullet says it too, the next day in "Paris 48": *"In front of the door of his miserable room, the only room in a ruin of a summerhouse. I saw the author of Théâtre et son Double and that I will never forget."*

I must add that there my brother was free to come and go, but at Rodez he wasn't. He was looked after at Rodez and forbidden drugs. He said to Jean Desterne "When I went into Dr. Ferdière's office and asked him for 25 drops of laudanum he said, "Not only will I not give you your 25 drops, but I will cure your craving with electro-shock treatment."

But at Ivry, as I've just said, he could come and go whenever he liked. He wasn't short of drugs, as he had found some amenable doctors in Paris . . .

93

And so it was that 18 months after leaving Rodez, Antonin Artaud was dying, alone, abandoned in a squalid room in a dilapidated and isolated summerhouse, full of chloral and laudanum! The "extremely precise goal" of the manifesto had been reached!

*   *   *

One word more about the manifesto.

Everybody knows that it had 170 signatures. But nobody knows that they were written on a skin of suffering.

In fact, since its publication some people—of considerable reputation—have come to tell me they regretted having signed. Even more came after the trial. They all had the same excuse. They signed without thinking, as if they were signing a book, without thinking. It never came into their heads that their signatures would be used for regrettable purposes.

So with each excuse another name was rubbed out. Today that list is reduced to none, because it only has the names of those I despise.

*   *   *

Naturally I must speak of Dr. Ferdière who also signed the manifesto, and accompanied it with a letter which appeared in the wretched pages of "Combat". Here is an extract: "It is a question of my fulfilling a simple duty towards the departed friend, the poet I admire, the artist I respect. So I put my name at the bottom of a manifesto which I agree with totally—and leave it to others to speculate on the meaning of my gesture. It is my way of replying officially to the stream of letters from Artaud's mother—those of his brother and sister are certainly 'posthumous'—and of letting her know which side I, in full possession of the facts, take." I am not surprised, for I am sure that Dr. Ferdière knows a lot of things.

He knows, for instance, that it was his friend, Robert Desnos, *pressed by the poet's mother,* who asked him to admit Antonin to the Rodez asylum.

He knows, too, that he *arbitrarily* accepted an abusive release-demand from the "Friends of the Poet".

He also knows that this was done without telling the poet's mother. And what is more *he knows* that he helped the libellers by saying that "The author's family were not interested in him and didn't come to see him at Rodez. That they never sent him any parcels."

But what Dr. Ferdière *does not know* is that he is amnesiac. Look at what he wrote to my mother on the 28th April 1943: "I advise you not to come and see him for the time being, travelling is so tiring . . . I take this opportunity to let you know that I had to refuse the last parcel you sent; it had been opened and eaten by rats. I advise you not to send any parcels for the time being . . ."

Incredible as it may be, it's true!

Later on he did not reply to the Poet's mother's stream of letters.

What had she written to him on 2 August, 1948?

Dear Doctor,

Very depressed by the premature death of my son Antonin Artaud. I have not been able to write to you before.

I know, whatever some people may say, that my son got much better while he was staying in your establishment, and I would like to express my gratitude for the trouble you have taken.

Sadly, when he was sent back too soon to a life which was no longer suitable for him and found himself in a harmful milieu, he couldn't help going back to the errors of his former life.

It is a sorrowful mother who asks you today to tell her how Antonin was when he left you, and why he left. There have been certain unpleasant suggestions about your behaviour and ours too, and I'm sure that your answer will help to establish the truth.

As everything my son possessed has disappeared in mysterious circumstances, I would be so grateful if you could tell me whether Antonin left anything, even if it has no value, at Rodez, because it would be a precious souvenir for me.

Also, about his literary work, as his circle made off with all the manuscripts he possessed when he died, I would like to ask you whether you had some of his papers and drawings which might complete the ones I already have.

Generally, the smallest detail about my son's life at Rodez would be useful to me. Do excuse me for causing you all this bother. I thank you in advance.

Yours faithfully,
(Signed) E. Artaud

One can see from this letter that the poet's mother deserved to be officially trampled on and that Dr. Ferdière, "in full possession of the facts," was quite right to take the side of the libellers.

And as I'm sure that Dr. Ferdière liked to be written about, here is a passage from a letter which A.A. wrote from Espalion, 3 May 1946, to his sister: " . . . And in the Rodez asylum I had 50 electric shock comas, it took away my memory and my consciousness for several months because Dr. Ferdière is a swine, and took heroin, wanted to get rid of me because he was jealous of my activity and my fertile spirit. That happens in life, the jealousy of an evil fool when he is ostensibly prodding a writer to start writing again. I'll tell you all about it when I see you."

And he did tell me all about it . . .

Now to reply to a little joke of Dr. Ferdière's in the letter I quoted above, it is right to add that the "certainly posthumous" sister really wants to come alive again, ten years later, just to give the Tour de Feu her personal authorization to publish the three letters addressed by her brother Antonin Artaud to the said Doctor.

I was not able to get the slightest idea of the way he was treated at the psychiatric Hospital of Rodez from the long discussions I had with my brother when he returned. I know that he was well treated. But when I asked him about it, he only laughed sarcastically.

I know that mental patients don't like their doctors. But my brother used to speak of Dr. Ferdière without any hate or anger. But with deep contempt, for he had very unpleasant memories.

That is all I can say . . . for the time being anyway.

However I assert that my brother was not cured when he left Rodez. And Dr. Ferdière *knows* that very well.

Do I have to prove it?

Here are two pieces of evidence. First, a letter from Dr. Ferdière, dated 23 May, 1945:

Madame,

I regret to inform you that unfortunately I do not share your optimism about the cure of Mr. Artaud. The prognosis of the disease is still serious. Perhaps one could attempt a trial release, but one cannot hope that the hallucinations and delirium will disappear completely. He will always need surveillance, and although it may one day be possible to do this in the outside world, it will always have to be extremely careful. At the moment he is going though another bad period. His physical health is good, but he is absorbed by his noxious experiences.

Yours sincerely,
Ferdière

Then this other letter of 18 Jan, 1946.

Madame,

Your opinion of the mental state of your son is painfully exact. His delirium is no better, on the contrary its scope grows wider. This does not cramp his literary activity: he is writing a lot. His physical health is good. So everything we have always thought is formally confirmed and there is little hope for a cure in the near future.

Yours sincerely,
For the Chief Doctor
Dequeker

Please note:
That this letter is dated the 18th January 1946 that three months later, May 3rd 1946, my brother wrote to me from Espalion: "... I am no longer at the Rodez asylum, my freedom was restored on Tuesday, 19 March, 1946 ... " and that a few weeks later, on the 25th May 1946, Dr. Ferdière signed the *poet's definite release!*
May I ask one question:
Whatever happened to all the manuscripts and drawings

which Antonin Artaud produced so prolifically at the Rodez psychiatric hospital?

And another question:

Perhaps you could tell me, Dr. Ferdière?

*   *   *

Ask in a St. Germain bookshop or a barrow-man on the Quais, in Paris or Jarnac, in France or abroad—as soon as you ask for the 2nd volume of the Complete Works of Antonin Artaud you will always everywhere, be told: "The author's family is opposing the publication."

But once a little bookshop clerk, who had some education, replied "His sister Isabelle has forbidden the publication of the 2nd volume." Everyone thought that Isabelle was Rimbaud's sister. No! I am Isabelle! Since the author's mother is dead, I am the head of the family; and so of course I am responsible for all the difficulties, the blocking and all the foolery which prevents the publication of this 2nd volume*.

As there are so many well-informed people in this world, there must be someone capable of giving formal and tangible proof of my opposition. AND I defy this someone to provide a letter or even a single word of mine which could constitute such a proof.

*   *   *

May I be allowed to say, that, on the subject of letters constituting formal and tangible proof, I have some myself. I ask you to do one the honour of believing me. But as I know that that is a lot to ask from some people, I will give an example to convince them. I speak to all those people who, maliciously or just from esprit-de-corps, have for more than ten years been the mouthpieces for patented libels.

Antonin Artaud didn't love his family.

Antonin Artaud had rejected his family.

Antonin Artaud had been abandoned by his family.

I say to all those people:

You are servile liars!

Because I can confound them, bringing irrefutable proofs

*   Finally published in France in 1961.

against their lies. And these proofs are the marks of profound affection which Antonin Artaud showed in countless letters to his family. First of all, there is one to his mother!

My dearest Maman,

I got your letter of the 6th of June and thank you for your birthday wishes.

Yesterday, June 21st, I got a letter from Marie-Ange, and she says I have a little money coming in, but I haven't been short of it. Anyway I don't need much here.

I've got an exit pass which allows me to go all round Rodez and I went specially to the Cathedral which is a miracle of the Middle Ages where you really enjoy praying and where I went specially for Holy Week. I prayed for all my family: you first of course, Marie-Ange, her children and Fernand.

I don't know when we will all see each other again but it would be right if life did a little for all of us and we were no longer separated by circumstances. It would be right above all, if life was more favourable to everybody for it has been too long that life has been practically impossible for all of us and GOD cannot like that. I have been out of the world for 7 years, since 1937 and I do not see when it will be mended. But the whole world suffers: I am interned but throughout the world people lack something: food or otherwise. GOD will provide! I knew that you had been tired and I made some vows for you to get well. We will all have better days. There are some people here amongst the Asylum personnel who are full of hope for me. That stops me despairing too much because it's been too many years that I've lacked too many things. But God will provide and will come back.

I embrace you with all my heart, Nanaqui.

Antonin Artaud

Here is another addressed to his sister:

My dearest Marie-Ange,

I got your letter of January 18th, and it gave me great
joy. But I don't think that I have written to you or Maman
since last October, or that I didn't acknowledge the receipt
of your mandate or else at least one of my letters must have
got lost.

A new printing of 1,725 copies of my book "Le Théâtre
et son Double" has just come out, the first edition of 300
which came out in 1938 has been out of print since then.
The publisher sent me 15 copies to distribute to my friends
and relations. I sent one to Maman the day before yesterday
and I would very gladly send you one if this book represented
my present ideas. But I no longer see things in the same way
since, in DUBLIN in September 1937 I went back to my
childhood faith and I have found a chapel in this asylum
and an almoner so that I can fulfill all my religious duties.
That book may not have anything specifically anti-religious
in it but it was written at a time of estrangement from and
disbelief in GOD and that comes through in more than one
passage and in these troubled times we are going through,
we need a passionate and energetic literature and when I
have prepared a specimen of such literature, able to lift up
the heart and soul of the reader, then I'll send it to you, and
you will be thankful to me, because you will find good for
you and yours. I have only one regret, reading this book I
wrote 8 years ago, and that is that all the literary dynamism
I had then was not used for more inspiring ideas. But that
will come.

I haven't yet received the parcel you told me about but
thank you for having thought of me. I asked for rye-bread
because I think you can get it without ration cards, and the
thing which I have missed most for several years is sweet
cakes or buns but I'm not forgetting that you have two
children who both need sugar and I beg you to give them all
they need before you think of me. I wonder whether Maman
and Fernand have got all they need, too. Tell Fernand when
you see him that despite my silence I think of him and pray

a lot for him. Give little Serg and Ghyslaine a kiss from me
and give George my regards. As for you, my dear Marie-Ange,
remember that whatever should happen to me I never forget
you and you can always count on my immutable love,
affection and all my heart.

> Nanaqui,
> Antonin Artaud

P.S. I've written to Maman by the same post.

And finally a third one to his niece, his sister's daughter.

> Rodez, 9 January, 1944

Yes my child, as you told your mother on Sunday with
such strength and spirit, I am not ill, but I have used these
six and a half years of confinement to meditate on my sins
and my faults, so as to correct myself and to eliminate them.
Anyway your mother has known all that for a long time in
her heart of hearts. But for so long now our hearts have been
closed to all, Ghyslaine, and we can no longer say what we
feel and think in the truth of our conscience and our life is
like a borrowed suit.

That is why, my child, you must not talk to me of illness.
It hurts me very much because it is not true. But there were
a lot of things to be put right in my behaviour and my
attitude to the world. I think that that is now done. For it
was principally a question of conscience. And the explana-
tion for all my sorrows is that before my journey to Ireland
I was thinking outside of God. God has given me strength
to look into myself and rid myself of Evil, for as you know
I came back to him in Dublin. And here at Rodez, there is a
chapel and an almoner in the asylum. I took communion
today for the feast of the Epiphany and I had a thought
especially for you, Ghyslaine, at the moment of that
communion. And God has given you too the strength to find
your own soul, for things in this world are heavy and difficult
and we do not always know where our soul is nor what it
wants. And if it could be applied to all the tasks of this
life. But it only needs a light from on High to enlighten us
on its real aspirations and its real capacities. God does not ask

much in return, did you know? A little thought, a little true prayer, and if we do not neglect all our duties in this life, then the will to intervene and support us.

Tell your Maman that I received her parcel, which I thank her for with all my heart and that I will write to her this week. But I've been in bed for three days with 'flu and a very high temperature and the almoner of the Asylum brought me communion in bed this morning, at my request, and as I said before, for the feast of the Epiphany.

I embrace you, my dear Ghyslaine, with all my great and deep affection.

Nanaqui.
Antonin Artaud.

P.S. Give Serge a kiss from me, as I know he wants me to come back to. He will see me again.

*　　　*　　　*

Are these letters not themselves the proof that my brother is not the sacrilegious poet whom some have tried to fix forever in his blasphemy?

I LOOKED AFTER ANTONIN ARTAUD

by Dr. Gaston Ferdière

One May night in 1958, about 2 or 3 o'clock, mulling over
Antonin Artaud's case once again and battling with a steak
which seemed rather badly disposed towards me, I thought of
the *Tour de Feu* and felt that I really must get in touch with
the Jarnac group. I felt this so strongly that I was just about to
pick up the phone and ask for Pierre Boujut's number: I
couldn't wait to find out what his reaction would be; but the
fear of looking ridiculous stopped me . . .

This first impulse was only put off for a few hours and
early in the morning I got through to Jarnac 119. Boujut's
voice gave me confidence straight away: he sounded very close;
his speech was slow and measured, rather lilting, agreeable. I
told him I was ringing from Bayonne, and I had to explain who
I was:

Yes, I'm a man with two lives!

He thought there were two of me and had never understood
that Gaston Ferdière, author of some poetry and critical pieces
he named, and Dr. Ferdière, psychiatrist and Artaud's doctor,
were one man . . .

His tone became more friendly, or at least I thought it did.
I explained quickly that I had finally decided to break my
ten-year silence, and that I had finally given in to my friends,
to Theodore Fraenkel whose letters were piling up, to Yonki
Desnos, and the others.

I told him what I wanted: I was looking for a free forum
dedicated to Artaud's memory, open for anyone to express
himself without constraint, to get to the bottom of the
problems, to ring the chime of truth! He immediately replied
that he found the idea extremely interesting, but he didn't run
the *Tour* single-handed and would have to ask his friends.

And thus the *consultation* took place at the *Tour de Feu Congress,* on the next 14th of July. I had arrived in Jarnac the evening before, about 10 o'clock, and joined the Tour people at Hillavet's on St. Simon, who were all in the dining room/ library, finishing dinner and reciting poems. I must have seemed awkward, cramped, rather boring; for a moment I wanted to resurrect an old guard-room habit and touch everyone on the shoulder. I said very little, and all evening I was subjected to criticism which the harsh red wine, the brandy, and the biscuits did little to ease.

    'We held at Jarnac the assizes of five'
said the Tour people in an Alexandrine which deserves a partner.

It was more of a *'Test by five'* for me, a rather painful trial: it was in the sparse shade of the island of St. Simon, in tall grass spared by the scythe; after a heavy picnic, eaten in the habitual discomfort of this sort of outing, a bit tipsy . . .

I talked for a long time, too long—an hour and a half, I'm told—and I hope that my listeners, sitting or lying on the ground, didn't sense my tiredness. I must say that their eyes, in which I constantly sensed new questions, encouraged me to go on, to go further and deeper.

*   *   *

Now, sitting at my desk, I miss the heat of St. Simon; I'm trying to recapture the mood on the bank of the Carente, the atmosphere of security, intellectual charity which I had gone there to find because I knew that I would find it there, nowhere else. The mood will not come back, direct, passionate, going beyond the words, fearing neither God nor Death. 'Things easily said have been hard to write' 'Isn't that G.M. Trevelyan (this historian admits that 'ease in the transition from one sentence to another has always come with the sweat of my brow').

*   *   *

Actually (these lines are written end of August '59) it does not seem to me that it is my personal task to comment or even write an epilogue—however briefly—but to record in brutal simplicity a certain number of facts which I consider of utmost importance, facts which are rigorously authentic, historically verifiable without the slightest difficulty, not themselves destined for discussion but merely to serve as a basis for discussion. I must make a real effort, contrary to my scientific training, not to enumerate dry roman or arabic figures, such as: (a) or (b), which, I must confess, have a tendency to slip into my exposition.

Let me start by saying: *it was not I who interned Antonin Artaud!* You cannot accuse me of breaking open an open door. I have read so often that I was the psychiatrist responsible for the arrest and imprisonment of Artaud, "the sod, the bastard who started it all". And I have seen the slander winkle its way in everywhere (at the Bayonne Court, in '57, the Government prosecutor Lafont tried to crush me, using anything which came to hand: "As for the administrative career of Dr. Ferdière," he said . . . "I must bring it to your attention: it is known that he . . . er . . . , arbitrarily imprisoned, er . . . a poet, er, a great poet . . . the poet Antonin . . . er" . . . a quick glance at his papers ends his hesitation and the orator swells his voice, trumpets "the poet Antonin Arnaud" (sic).

The truth is that *Antonin Artaud was officially committed more than 5 years before we first met.* The date of the certificate, giving his entry to the St. Anne Clinical Asylum is 12 April, 1938. He was transferred to Ville Evrard on the 27th February, 1938. He was to stay there until the 22nd January 1943.

I did not begin to take an interest in Artaud until November '42. Of course I knew from the beginning that he had to be interned, and I knew why. I had discussed it several times with friends such as Guita and Theodore Fraenkel, Jean-Louis Barrault, Léon Pierre-Quint etc. . . .

You, Ferdière, you should do something!

Do what? I didn't see that I had any responsibility to take the poet's fate in hand. In the autumn of 1942 I decide, at the insistence of a generous man called Robert Desnos, who I was very fond of, let alone our many mutual likes (for naive art, children's paintings, glass, Third Empire post cards . . .). In fact I get a real S.O.S. from Desnos: "Artaud always upset, is spending long spells in 'security wing' of Ville Evrard; he gets nothing to eat, his condition is deteriorating, is dangerously thin" . . . If you remember, it was the terrible time of food restrictions, ration books and black market; in the asylums psychopaths are virtually condemned to death by Nazism:

they suffer terrible sores; thousands die of hunger. We decide not to let Artaud die, to class him among those who must be saved at any price. We let the family and his faithful friends know; *don't go thinking that you couldn't count them on one hand;* headed by the most zealous—Jean Paulhan, Paul Eluard.

I don't intend to give all the details of how Desnos and I, after long efforts, managed to arrange *the transfer from Ville Evrard to Rodez,* then in the 'free zone'. Here is an inter-zone letter from Desnos, stamped the 26 January, 1943.

My Dear Ferdière,

I went to Ville Evrard on Thursday, Artaud was supposed to go the next day, Friday 22. I found him raving in delirium, talking like St. Jerome and not wanting to go, because he would be separated from favourable magical forces. I had not seen him for 5 years—his exaltation and his madness were a painful sight. I have persuaded his mother not to pay attention to what he says, to let him go, so sure am I that he will improve with you. But he seems well settled in his fantasies and difficult to cure.

Desnos

Artaud will certainly think of me as his persecutor!

Doesn't this letter say everything in a few lines? Without mentioning the post-script which I leave my detractors to think about.

This is not the place to discuss the diagnosis of Artaud's psychosis . . . All I want to establish here is that *there was delirium, chronic delirium, and that this delirium made Artaud violently anti-social, a danger to public order and to people's safety.* I use those words voluntarily, these ready-made words, words of law and custom, which society has assembled for its own defence. At Boujut's request I add here a topical example of Artaud's derangement, the dedication of 'Nouvelles Revelations de l'Etre' to the Führer. One recognizes in this passage the false memory (so frequent in Artaud) the mystic ideas, the glossotalia etc. . . .

106

To Adolf Hitler
in memory of
the Romanisches café in
Berlin one afternoon
in May 1932
and because I pray
God to give you the
grace to re-remember
all the marvels
which HE (sic) you that
day the GRATIFIED
(RESUSCITATED)
        THE HEART
Kudar dayro Zarish Ankkara Thabi
        Antonin Artaud
        3 Dec 1943

Artaud's religious conviction changed every week, or every day. The people who discuss his convictions with such certainty make me laugh. Before they reach for their pens and put up the scaffolding of their theses, they would do well to speak to the almoner at Rodez. The poor man never knew whether Artaud would come to services to pray or scream abuse at him. My wife was always taken for a saint and Mrs. Latrémolière, my intern's wife, was thought to be possessed by the devil—like most women, by the way—whom he would exorcise in passing, by hawking, sneezing and spitting.

A little correction to another widespread misconception. Artaud was not committed as a drug-addict.

He certainly took drugs, occasionally like many artists and surrealists. He was certainly not an addict. The clinical type of his delirium showed no signs of an addiction. I never noticed the craving for drugs in him. And it was so easy for me and my interns to deceive him. In reply to his continual demand for codeine, we would give him a couple of drops of codoforme which would, at most, soothe his smoker's cough (a smoker who was certainly unaware of tobacco rationing).

I must add something, weighing my words carefully:

I say that ARTAUD was turned into a real addict by his friends at the end, his newly-acquired friends, many of whom were addicts. They hastened his end with large doses of laudanum. One has good grounds for thinking that but for their stupid interference and their complacency, Artaud would have given us a much more substantial body of work.

*   *   *

For I had certainly not 'cured' Artaud and he was really incurable with the present resources of psychiatric therapy. And I don't understand what the words 'cure' and 'mental health' mean in relation to such an exceptional man.

At least I returned Artaud to society on 25 May, 1946. At least, and most important of all, *I had returned him to artistic and poetic creation.*

Yes, I can say calmly and without false modesty, without me, Artaud would have died sterile: without me, the famous 'Lettres de Rodez' and 'Van Gogh' would never have seen the light!

What did I do to obtain this result?

I need not account to anyone, even my psychiatric colleagues—until I judge it right to do so.

I will not go into the value of seismotherapy here, or the role which a few sessions of electric shock treatment played in Artaud's case. However I must hammer in a nail that has already been driven home: E.C.T. is absolutely painless—contrary to the assertions of romantics and journalists short of copy. The awakening may be accompanied by manifestations of anxiety, just at the moment of regaining consciousness and reconstructing the personality; anyway it was only of this moment that Artaud complained in violent terms, during that lecture at the Vieux Colombier which terrified the audience and caused so much ink to flow.

I have also been accused of using E.C.T. as a punishment. You know how it goes;

M. Artaud, give up magic, or I'll give you the E.C.T.!

Or like this:

M. Artaud, your last poem is incomprehensible! Write clearly, write poetry like everybody else, or I will make you start E.C.T. again!

It's really a bit much and really too stupid! It's beyond belief that there could be such Parissots (Parissot: editor-publisher and friend of Artaud) as to believe it; everyone who knows me and has seen me work is outraged by such suggestions.

After all, E.C.T. could not do much in this type of psychosis if it were used in isolation. Especially if I had not always treated Antonin Artaud with the greatest consideration and the greatest humanity. *Was it not human dignity* that had to be restored to this internee of long standing, sunk in asylum or prison habits?

I was waiting for him when the ambulance brought him to the hospital, on that first morning, and held out my hand. He threw himself in my arms, as if he'd found his dearest friend; as if we'd known each other for 15 or 20 years; mentioning a dozen mutual friends whose names I'd never heard, chanting a litany of false memories which I was careful not to correct. I told him about my plan to return him to freedom, life, the world of art and letters and took him to lunch at my house. My wife was very kind. She welcomed him with open arms, let herself be hugged by this man whose appearance was repulsive. It is painful for the mistress of a house to have a guest who grunts and shoves food into his mouth, rubs food into the tablecloth, belches, spits on the floor, and, before the end of the meal, kneels down to sing psalms. I calmed him by returning to him a little demascene sword, such as you buy in the market at Toledo, which I found in his belongings.

*   *   *

The result I obtained, which would have amazed and delighted poor Desnos if he could have seen it, was largely due to Art-Therapy. I am recognized as one of the pioneers in this field and I have defined and explained it at a great number of meetings and congresses. *Artaud's hand had to relearn how to write*, by means of the increasingly heavy correspondence he conducted with his friends (at the beginning he had to be urged to reply even a short note, full of cliches); most of all, through the translations I asked him to do for me as a friend, as a favour, something I needed, for some piece of work or other, an adaptation of a Lewis Carroll poem or a whole chapter of "Through the Looking Glass." So one day, without letting on, I sent Southwell's 'The Fire Baby' (Le Bébé de Feu) to Pierre Seghers and a few months later, in 'Poetry 44', Artaud could see his own work in black and white; this, after years of

109

obscurity and silence; his joy was tremendous; I saw his face light up; he re-read the lines with visible satisfaction; the ply seemed to have worked.

Let the fools who blame me for preventing the publication of Artaud's work while he was in Rodez ask the opinion of Pierre Seghers, or of Marc Barbézat of 'L'Arbalete' or of Marcel Béalu.

And Seghers, Barbézat and Béalu will have something to say about my deep respect of the poetry—for I am sure, you remember the fable publicised by "Revue K": the psychiatrist 'normalizing' Artaud's poetry, trying to impose his own taste and canons . . .

Ah! I implore you, *don't let the paper merchants "play with poetry"!*

For I forbade a paper merchant by the name of Henri Parissot to publish the 'Letters from Rodez'. And not only had I the right, but also the duty, to do so. The Act of 1838 has certain fixed provisions. In particular, it protects the rights of the insane committed under its authority, and provides them, on the day of their committal, with an administrator of the goods and estate of the insane! (I apologize for these details, they are essential.) In 1946, the 'administrator of the goods and estate of the insane' of Rodez psychiatric hospital was called Maître (Lawyer) Périquoi. If he was still alive, he could recount our long conversations about the eventual publication of 'Letters from Rodez' and the decisions which we felt obliged to take to protect the financial interests of Antonin Artaud. He would also tell you that no publisher's contract was submitted, a contract which only he could sign in the name of our patient.

*　　　*　　　*

Artaud's hand also had to relearn how to draw.

We provided him with paper and pencils of all sorts. At first his lack of skill was touching, infantile; then his sureness of touch and his courage increased, thanks to my and Delanglade's encouragement. He was always tearing up his work; I rescued a self-portrait from destruction. I told him sincerely that I was interested in it; after a short reflection, he gave it to me.

*　　　*　　　*

It took a long time to prepare Artaud's release. I wanted him to be released under the best possible conditions and before I approached the administrative authorities I had to assemble a certain number of guarantees. History has shown that I was not strict enough, and, if I feel any regrets, they are on this point.

The financial question was solved by the matinée at the Sarah Bernhardt Theatre which brought in more than a million. This is not the place to thank all those who took part, who offered money or works to be sold etc. . . .

I insisted that as soon as he got to Paris, Artaud should be put in a private clinic so that he could be fed regularly and not left to himself and his unfortunate personal habits. A guardian angel was found. Not the one I would have chosen. But I did not want to insist.

*   *   *

I went to Paris with Artaud, we took the evening train from Rodez. The memory of that night still tears at my heart. Before dawn we abandoned our couchettes and stood in the corridor. Leaning on the copper bar we chain-smoked and had a friendly, not to say, affectionate, conversation. I felt Artaud's deep attachment to me, his confidence in me, and his worries about the future. I certainly gave him some last advice, and enveloping myself in oratorical devices which did not deceive Artaud, I sketched vague Damoclean swords . . . My brother psychoanalists will doubtless laugh at my 'paternalism'. I would like to have seen them in my place!

On the platform at Austerlitz Station, a group of Artaud's friends was waiting, preparing declarations and embraces.

I was soon surprised at their haste to leave him. One man said he was very tired; another had to rush off to an important engagement; another did not like the idea of a taxi-ride with Artaud, and was rather frightened (this charity is quite unlike me, I name no names!)

We parted with a handshake. But it was my turn to feel anguish and I felt my eyelids moisten.

*   *   *

I have said nothing about *Artaud's family*, that family which I rather stupidly called 'posthumous' one day when I was angry

111

with them. I wasn't angry with them for not sending parcels.
They knew he lacked for nothing and they had stayed in occupied
Paris. I was rather angry with them for not helping me about
Artaud's clothes. Above all, it seems to me that his sister could
have found time in 3 years and 3 months to come and see him.
I mainly accuse the Artaud family for misunderstanding his
work and genius *while he was alive.* So you see what I meant
by my little joke. (i.e. posthumous)

*   *   *

A story to end with:
In 1948, I organise an exhibition of so-called pathological
art, and I am going to preside at the opening.
A petition circulates in the Latin Quarter, at St. Germain—
des-Prés; drawn up by Camille Bryen, I think, and directed
against me, warning me to withdraw Artaud's paintings from
the exhibition.
Wait for it: there is nothing of Artaud's in the exhibition,
and there was never any question of hanging any of his work.
However the petition had already collected quite a few
signatures (well, well!)
I find Bryden on the Quai des Grands Augustines, between
two barrows. He seems dumb-struck, opens his eyes wide
behind his round spectacles, sucks in his cheeks . . . and runs
off.

*   *   *

P.S. Well, now the discussion has begun!
Question me, that's all I ask, I who would have had so
many questions to ask Hölderlin's, Nerval's, Nietzche's, and
Van Gogh's doctors!